942·67 REF COLL

THE

STANSTED

EXPERIENCE

by

John F. Hamlin

published by GMS Enterprises

in association with The Aero Book Co.
P.O. Box 1045, Storrington, West Sussex

THE STANSTED EXPERIENCE

First published 1997
by GMS Enterprises
67 Pyhill, Bretton,
Peterborough,
England PE3 8QQ
Tel and Fax (01733) 265123

ISBN: 1 870384 56 3

Printed and bound for GMS Enterprises by
Woolnough Ltd, Express Works, Irthlingborough, Northants

BIBLIOGRAPHY

"Action Stations" (Vol. 1) — Michael J. F. Bowyer (Patrick Stephens, 1979)
Aircraft Illustrated magazine
"Air Force Combat Units of World War II" — M. Maurer (US Govt. Printing Office, 1961)
"Avro Aircraft Since 1908" — A. J. Jackson (Putnam, 1965)
"British Civil Aircraft" (Parts 1, 2 and 3) — A. J. Jackson (Putnam)
"Control Towers" — Paul Francis (Airfield Research Publishing, 1993)
The Daily Express newspaper
"Handley Page Aircraft Since 1907" — C. H. Barnes (Putnam, 1976)
"Permission To Land" — B. Cashinella & K. Thompson (Arlington Books, 1971)
Archival material provided by Reg. Robinson
"Royal Air Force Burtonwood" — A. P. Ferguson (Airfield Publications, 1989)
"Support & Strike" — J. F. Hamlin (GMS Enterprises, 1991)
The Daily Telegraph newspaper
The Times newspaper

Contents

Introduction

Surely no major British airport has had a more difficult, more traumatic existence than Stansted? Since the heady days of post-war air freighting which established the civilian airport, several attempts have been made to minimise its use, or even close it entirely, but all such attempts have been matched by an equal number of efforts to expand its activity as a viable commercial enterprise. At the time of writing, however, London Stansted Airport, with its new terminal building, enlarged cargo facilities and business aviation centre, seems set fair to grow within prescribed limits over the next few years.

Following its construction in 1942/43 by the US Army, Stansted airfield was used intensively by the US 9th Air Force for about two years before being taken over by the Royal Air Force as a storage and disposal depot. While the RAF was still using the premises, the first civilian airlines began to fly from Stansted, setting a precedent for others to follow. The 1950s and 1960s were decades of mixed fortunes for users of Stansted, who came and went according to the demands and the financial climate of the time. They were hindered by poor passenger-handling arrangements at Stansted, which were not modernised until 1969. From that point matters gradually improved, although even then there were set-backs. It was not until Stansted was designated as London's third airport in 1985 and the decision was made that a new terminal would be built that passenger business really began to increase.

Since the opening of the new facilites in 1991, passenger figures have shown a remarkable increase, and several airlines are operating scheduled services within the UK and to European destinations from Stansted. Much time and money has been spent on ensuring that, as far as possible, environmental considerations are handled properly, and the result is an airport fit for further expansion into the 21st century.

In compiling this book, I have received help from a number of people, who I have listed below. My sincere thanks go to them and to any others whom I may have omitted inadvertantly.

John F. Hamlin, May 1997

ACKNOWLEDGEMENTS

Lambert Austin and Carl M. Christ: Historians of the 344th Bomb Group, US 9th Air Force.
Brian Cone: formerly of the CAA Flying Unit.
Vic 'Dinkie' Curtis: an airfield worker from April 1944.
Jack Cutmore: an airframe fitter with LAMS from late 1947.
Sqn. Ldr. Bert Edgerley: a navigator with LAMS
Carol A. Hancocks: Customer Services Superintendent, Servisair (UK) Ltd.
Phil Kemp, Nigel Kemp, Ian Bird, Derek Harknett and others of the Stansted Branch of Air Britain for their practical support.
Sir Peter G. Masefield MA C.Eng Hon.DSc Hon.DTech Hon.FRAeS FCIT Hon.FAIAA (USA) Hon.FCASI Hon.FIRTE FRSA: former Chairman of British Airports Authority.
Peter McLean: Operations Manager, Stansted Airport Ltd.
Sheena Harrison, Marketing, Air UK Ltd.

Norman Mead: Chairman, North-West Essex & East Herts. Preservation Association.
George O'Neal, Linda Keightley, Catherine Stott, and Dave Mason of NATS.
Capt. Keith Moody.
Mrs. Yvonne Sintes (formerly Mrs. Yvonne Pope).
Ron Paternoster: Operations Director, Stansted Airport Ltd.
Reg. Robinson, for his invaluable help.
Graham M. Simons: my publisher, for his valued advice and for writing many of the captions.
Bryan Southgate: Head of Public Relations, FLS Aerospace Ltd.
Kevin Topham: ex 263 MU, RAF Stansted Mountfitchet.
John Williams: Head of Public Affairs, Stansted Airport Ltd.
Judith Slater and Deana Frost, Public Affairs, BAA Stansted.

Unless otherwise captioned, photographs in this history were supplied by Reg. Robinson, mostly from the collection of the late Peter Pallet.

Foreword

by Sir Peter G. Masefield

In the long and chequered histories of modern airports throughout the world, none has been more varied, more turbulent, more beset with political vacillations, public debate, local concern, present achievement and future promise than has Stansted Airport in Essex, the third and latest of the three London airports.

In this well-written book, meticulously researched by John F. Hamlin, Stansted's remarkable evolution is traced through the 55 years since it came on to the wartime aviation scene in July 1942. Mr. Hamlin tells its evocative story, blow-by-blow, from the time when its runways were laid down by engineers of the US Army as a medium bomber base for the US Army Air Force to its present flourishing status as London's third airport .

I commend it most warmly to all students of the extraordinary history of the endeavours of successive national governments, local authorities and numerous committees to find a solution to national requirements for the conflicting interests of international air transport, national economics, local people and modern technology. It took 42 years to come to an agreed basis for the long-term future of Stansted.

This book comes at a significant and welcome time in our national and international air transport affairs, when a crisis looms concerning the ability of the four runways at Heathrow, Gatwick and Stansted to meet steadily-growing traffic requirements up to and beyond the first decade of the 21st century. This will only partly be resolved by a long-awaited go-ahead for the construction of much-needed Terminal 5 at Heathrow.

Despite helpful advances in air traffic control techniques, the increase in average size of aircraft and competition from the Channel Tunnel, few unused runway 'slots' are now available at Heathrow and Gatwick; certainly not at desirable hours, nor even at most of the less desirable times of year. There is little prospect of more slots in the London area, other than at Stansted.

For years past there has been a surprising lack of concern about this impending — and now present — shortage of runway capacity at the two foremost London airports. Such a lack of foresight has existed in Government circles ever since the two additional runways originally planned for Heathrow, north of the Bath Road, were abandoned in 1953, together with Gatwick's

planned second runway and the original concept of a four-runway airport at Stansted. Instead, in 1985, came the re-affirmation of Stansted as yet another major single-runway airport. It was at least — and at last — a substantial step forward.

Given the obvious need to provide for the future, as the demands of international air traffic are likely to double at least every dozen years, some cardinal facts stand out in the course of more than half a century of Stansted history covered by this book.

Firstly, we owe the fact that we have a third London airport, capable of reasonable access and essential development, to the United States, which not only laid out the runway system at their 'Station 169' in 1943 but also saved the embryo Stansted Airport from being closed and dismantled by the Ministry of Civil Aviation between 1953 and 1957. Instead it was retained for use by the US Strategic Air Command should a need arise for additional NATO forces to be based in Great Britain against potential Russian threats. By contrast, in a White Paper of July 1953 the Minister of Civil Aviation, Alan Lennox Boyd, stated that *"....civil flying will stop at Northolt, Bovingdon and Stansted, and Croydon will be sold"*. Only Gatwick, a grass airfield, would be retained as a bad-weather alternate for Heathrow, but would not be used intensively all year round. That was the lowest ebb in the complex story of London's airports, at a time of failure by Ministers to recognise the growing importance of air transport to the economic future and well-being of the United Kingdom.

A second issue, among the many complexities of the Stansted Airport story, is the conglomeration of often conflicting, controversial and lengthy Government White Papers, reports of public enquiries and Statements of Case, seventeen in all, which came to be assembled and debated around London airports' policies and politics. They have taken up an infinite number of man-years and continue to do so.

A single runway at Gatwick was opened in May 1958. Ten years later, when capacity at the London airports was clearly under serious pressure, the Roskill Commission was convened "to enquire into the need for a four-runway airport to cater for the growth of traffic at existing airports serving the London area, to consider the various alternative sites and to recommend which should be selected". The Commission was presided over by the distinguished future Lord Roskill of Newtown, who was asked to take special account of a detailed cost / benefit analysis.

After three years of well-intentioned deliberations, the industrious Roskill Commission arrived at the wrong answers on every count. Astonishingly, having quickly ruled out Stansted, with its valuable upgraded runway, the Commission produced a short-list of four sites for a "new approach" to a third London airport. They were at Cublington in Buckinghamshire, Foulness (on Maplin Sands, off Foulness Island in the Thames Estuary), Nuthampstead in Hertfordshire and Thurleigh, near Bedford, all more than 40 miles from London. With work on Stansted abandoned, the Commission's majority recommendation in 1971 was for Cublington as the third London airport. It was accompanied by a minority vote in favour of Foulness, which was by far the most distant and expensive site.

Impressed by the labours and erudition of the Commission, Sir Edward Heath's Conservative government announced in April 1971 that it accepted the minority report for Maplin on environmental grounds, and in 1973 set up a Development Authority to reclaim Maplin Sands, only for that decision, fortunately, to be overturned in March 1974 by the succeeding Labour government under Harold Wilson on grounds of spiralling cost. A new 'Maplin Review' was set up to re-assess dates and requirements.

Relevant to all this was the exasperated and cogent statement of the Secretary of State for Trade in Margaret Thatcher's Conservative government, the Rt. Hon. Edmund Dell, when in December 1979 he wrote that on airport policies *"...years of indecision and counter-decision reflect no credit on this country's capacity to make difficult but necessary choices"*.

Notwithstanding these remarks, yet another Public Enquiry was launched under the practical Graham Eyre QC in December 1980. In his report of April 1984 he emphasised the need for *"the taking of decisive action to provide a sufficiency of effective and efficient airport capacity throughout the UK and in the London airports system as a whole"*.

With some urgency (by contrast with so much that had gone before), the (now) Sir Graham Eyre recommended that Stansted should be reinstated (for the third time) as London's third airport, that it should be provided with terminal capacity for up to 15 million passengers per year, a high quality rail link and further provision for up to 25 million passengers, while a fifth terminal should be built at Heathrow.

As it happened, this vindication of Stansted's potential was almost exactly forty years after I had first flown into and out of Stansted's then incomplete airfield as co-pilot of a B-17 Fortress bomber of the 96th Bomb Group of the US 8th Air Force, with which I had been flying on active service on 'liaison day bombing' missions. Thereafter, the way of the world brought me, between 1966 and 1972, to be Chairman of British Airports Authority, newly-formed to own and operate Stansted, Heathrow, Gatwick, Prestwick, Edinburgh and Glasgow Airports.

Twenty years later, after substantial progress, as recorded in the pages which follow, BAA invested a further £400 million to provide Stansted with a new, thoroughly modern passenger terminal which, with other developments, have placed it in the forefront of airport amenities anywhere in the world. By the spring of 1997 Stansted was handling over five million passengers per year.

Many salutary lessons can be learned from Stansted's long apprenticeship and its eventual confirmation as London's third airport. As Mr. Hamlin shows, Stansted approaches the 21st century as Europe's fastest-growing airport. It is becoming increasingly important internationally through its exceptional prospects for development and its ability to bring better communications, useful employment and wider prosperity to a pleasant and still under-developed part of London's countryside. Further reduction in aircraft noise and substantial moves towards cleaner emissions will enable airports to become better neighbours, not least at Stansted, where careful environmental planning, better surface access and attractive architecture continue to be the order of the day.

And so, after many tribulations, here at Stansted, in Graham Greene's words *"A door opens and lets the future in"* .

Peter G. Masefield, May 1997

Chapter One

George Washington Field

During the early part of the Second World War, the residents of the north-west Essex village of Stansted Mountfitchet saw little first-hand evidence of the rapidly-increasing Allied airborne campaign. The only well-established airfield in the immediate vicinity was Sawbridgeworth, six miles to the south-west, which had been in use intermittently before the war and constantly since 1940 by army co-operation squadrons of the RAF, flying Lysanders and single-seat Tomahawks and Mustangs. RAF Hunsdon, located beyond Sawbridgeworth, had been used from May 1941 by Hurricane and Havoc squadrons, and no doubt some of these aircraft were seen in the local skies.

The situation was about to change, however, in a way that could never have been envisaged by those involved. On 14 July 1942, the first elements of the 817th Engineer Aviation Battalion, US Army, arrived from the United States, from where they had sailed on the USS *Argentina,* to begin work on a new airfield to accommodate a Strategic Air Depot of the US 8th Air Force. To be located on the flat plateau just east of Stansted Mountfitchet, the airfield had been designed to Class A standards, and was to

be laid out in the usual triangular pattern of three runways. Four-man tents were pitched for the new arrivals by members of the 815th EA Bn. who had come from Northern Ireland specially, and after potatoes had been lifted from the fields by girls of the Women's Land Army the American engineers were soon hard at work clearing trees and hedges from the site and laying out a drainage system, using the mechanical equipment with which the US Army was liberally equipped. As soon as the site was clear and the engineers had surveyed the ground for the runways and perimeter tracks, concreting began. In addition, work began on domestic buildings, principally Nissen barrack huts and associated facilities, on the western side of the site to accommodate the large number of men expected to be based on the new airfield. At this stage, the embryo airfield was named, unofficially, George Washington Field, and, even more unofficially, Kurstedt Field, after the Battalion's Commander, Col. Harold A. Kurstedt. [Only one of the several American-built airfields in Great Britain received an American-style title: Andrews Field, located at Great Saling. It is assumed that the British Air Ministry did not much approve of the idea!]. Also

A Blaw-Knox concrete-laying 'train' used by the Aviation Engineer Batallions of the US Army on runway construction in England. At the time this was much more modern than the equipment used by the British construction companies. [D. Benfield]

Let building work commence!
Above: Men of the 850th EAB starting work on the construction
of a hangar at Stansted in 1943
Right: Here a tracked crane is seen hoisting roof elements
into place. Note the erection team up in the rafters!
[M. Marshaw]

Below: The driver of a Caterpillar D.8 tractor stands by his
machine at Stansted during the construction of the airfield.

working on the site was a local contracting company, Ashton's, whose men helped the American engineers to carry out the task even more rapidly. To give some refreshment to the hard-working construction personnel, a local dairy sent a milkmaid to the site with a milk-cart from which milk could be ladled into mess-tins, but this enterprise was soon stopped by the British War Department, who complained that if the service wasn't provided on British-manned sites it wouldn't be on those of the Americans!

While the American engineers were at Stansted, social activities were enjoyed by all concerned. In August 1942 a social evening and dance was held in Long's Restaurant, Bishops Stortford, with admission by invitation only due to the expected large demand. Mr. E.F.Cooper, the President of the local Chamber of Trade,

opened the proceedings by welcoming the newly-arrived American servicemen and Lt. Nackles spoke in appreciation of this welcome. A USAAF band provided the music, and the whole event was greatly enjoyed by local people and Americans alike. Saturday-night dances at Long's became a regular feature of life during this period, and Anglo-American relations were developed to the extent that it was often difficult for the servicemen to be present at 'Reveille' next morning! The 817th EA Bn's own group, *The Jive Bombers',* gave shows on a wooden stage in a field close to their tented domestic site and played weekly at a nearby Land Army camp and a hospital. There was also a Drum and Bugle Corps formed of men of the 817th.

In late September 1942, by which time the runways and perimeter tracks were about half

GEORGE WASHINGTON FIELD

Right: A tracked concrete mixer with loading bucket, part of the first batch of construction equipment for use at Stansted is transhipped onto road vehicles near Stansted Mountfitchet railway station in the summer of 1942.

Below: In the centre of Bishops Stortford, at the junction of High St. and North St., a USAAF GI poses with a British 'bobby' for a photo to send to the folks back home, watched with some amusement by a pair of soldiers on the extreme right.

completed, the 817th EA Bn. was relieved of duty at Stansted so that the men could begin a period of further training to fit them for service in North Africa. The 817th was replaced by the 825th EA Bn., which carried on with work on the runways and roads and began construction of the control tower, fire station and motor transport section. By November 1942, most of two of the runways had been completed and work on roads and Nissen huts which in due course would be occupied by

the 344th Bomb Group was well advanced. On 10 November the 817th EA Bn., their training completed, left the Essex site to begin the long journey to Oran in Algeria.

Almost certainly the first aircraft to attempt to land at Stansted was an RAF Stirling, BF445 of 214 Squadron, based at Chedburgh in Suffolk. Returning from an operation on Nurenburg on 26 February 1943, the pilot of this four-engined aircraft, which was short of fuel, decided to attempt a landing at Stansted, only to find the almost-complete runways obstructed. During the enforced overshoot, the Stirling hit the trees of Stocking Wood at Thremhall Priory, near the southern boundary of the airfield, and came to a sudden halt! The aircraft was destroyed, but there seem to have been no serious injuries to the crew.

Next to join the ever-growing number of personnel at Stansted was the 850th EA Bn., which arrived by train on 20 May 1943 from Gourock in Scotland, where their ship from the USA had docked. After being carried by trucks of the 825th EA Bn. to their Nissen hut living quarters, the first they had seen, the men were served with their *"...first decent meal for two weeks"*. They quickly began work on their first project - the base hospital, working ten-hour shifts, six days per week, with the seventh day allocated for training. During the few hours of leisure they did enjoy, a popular place was 'The Barley Mow' pub at Stansted Mountfitchet, where mild and bitter could be bought.

The next task for the 850th was the communal site and recreation centre on the new Tactical Air

Domestic and Admin. sites of the 344th BG at Stansted.

Each domestic site contained a number of Officer's and Sergeant's Quarters and Airmen's Barracks, along with the Latrines, Ablution Blocks and a Drying Room.

The Communal Site contained a Ration and Grocery Store, Institute (the famous 'PX'), Tailor's, Barber's and Shoemaker's Shops Gymnasium and Squash Court.

Within the Administration Site were the Station Offices (including the office of RAF Liaison Officer), Operations Building, Crew Briefing Room, and the Bomb Sight repair and storage building.

The Mess Site was home of the C.O.'s Quarters, Officers and Sergeants Messes and a Dining Room for 800 Airmen. Here also was the Showers and Boiler House.

The Sick Quarters had a 22-bed hospital, Dental Surgery, Mortuary and Ambulance garage.

All-in-all the 'Dispersed Sites' were a self-contained town.

DISPERSED SITES

Site No.3 · Site No.2 · Site No.6 · Liitle Drury Lodge · Anti-Aircraft HQ site · Bury Lodge · Duck End Farm · Communal site · Administration Site · WAAF site · Mess Site No.1 · Sick Qtrs site · Site No.1 · Site No.4 · Site No.5

Depot complex, located on the north-eastern side of the airfield, work on which began in July 1943. No days off were allowed for the first three weeks, but after that Sundays were free, and passes were issued allowing the men to visit Cambridge and London. Very soon, foundations were being laid for hangars, and the MT park and roads were under construction, as were large numbers of barrack huts of several types. By August 1943, the project was sufficiently complete to be useable, and elements of the 2nd Tactical Air Depot, which was to be the resident unit, began to move in on 17 August. The hard-working men of the 850th EA Bn. enjoyed the opening of their Red Cross Club and organised a dance to celebrate the first anniversary of the activation of their Battalion.

By this time, although no facilities such as air traffic control or crash rescue yet existed at Stansted, aircraft had began to visit! Possibly the first aircraft to land, Boeing B-17F 42-30160 *'Dallas Rebel'* of the 96th Bomb Group, piloted by Capt. John Nance, touched down amidst the piles of building materials at heaps of spoil on 6 July 1943. Flying as Co-Pilot on board was Mr Peter Masefield, then a war correspondent accredited to both the RAF and US 8th Air Force. He again flew into the embryo airfield on 24 July, this time in B-17F 42-29945 *'Daisy June IV'*, with Capt Al Lambert as pilot. The reasons behind these visits, both from Snetterton Heath in Norfolk, was a pragmatic one - East Anglian-based aircrews quickly discovered that when they were not needed for operations, their most convenient route to the metaphorically-speaking 'bright lights of London' was via Stansted! Little did Mr (later Sir) Peter Masefield realise at the time that he would be closely associated with Stansted in later years as Chairman of the British Airports Authority.

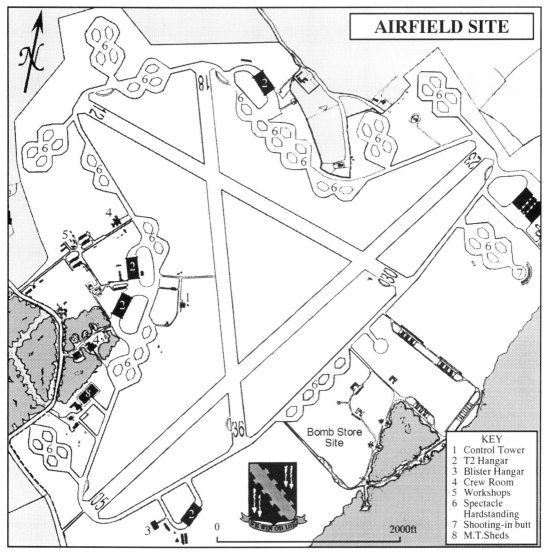

AIRFIELD SITE

KEY
1 Control Tower
2 T2 Hangar
3 Blister Hangar
4 Crew Room
5 Workshops
6 Spectacle
  Hardstanding
7 Shooting-in butt
8 M.T.Sheds

Bomb Store
Site

2000ft

By 8 September 1943, the 825th EA Bn. had moved from the airfield site to assist the 850th working on the TAD site, and was employed in the erection of a number of 'American' huts. Hardstandings on the TAD site were sixty per cent complete by mid-September, and the arrival of the 816th EA Bn. from Gosfield on 11 October helped matters along considerably, although this unit stayed at Stansted only until 23 December before moving on to another site at Boreham. Dedication of the airfield site took place on 16 October 1943, and the base, now designated USAAF Station 169, was assigned to the US Ninth Air Force as the 2nd Tactical Air Depot, which controlled, from time to time, a number of Air Depot Groups.

An interested spectator to all the work was Jim Carter, a submariner who was home on leave late in 1943. Seeing Jim looking through the hedge, an American serviceman gave him a conducted tour of the new base and 200 cigarettes when he left!

Thanksgiving Day, in November 1943, was celebrated by the men leaving work at 16.00 hours instead of 18.00, and then enjoying a dinner of Turkey, dressing, cranberry sauce, ice cream, cake and apple pie. By now, the weather was becoming poor, and the dust of the summer was turning into mud. Equipment was wearing out, and spare parts were difficult to obtain, but the work was almost finished, and at the end of the year the airfield itself was regarded as being

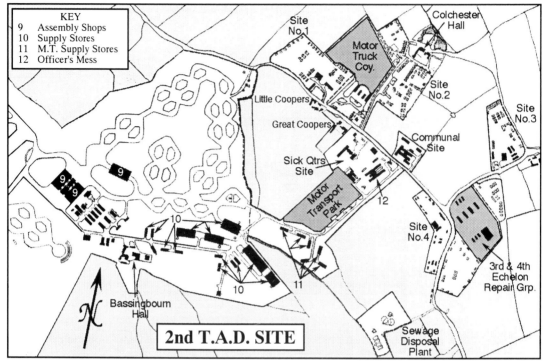

KEY
9   Assembly Shops
10 Supply Stores
11 M.T. Supply Stores
12 Officer's Mess

2nd T.A.D. SITE

'operational'. Only a half-day break was allowed for Christmas festivities, however, as the urgency was to complete all outstanding work. Hangars and ancillary buildings were ready for use, and work was beginning on the boiler house and the 60ft (18m.) water tower. However, during the Christmas period, Essex County Council presented a large leather chair, emblazoned with the County seal, to Maj. Grimm, although the reason for this is not recorded. During the same few days, a six-ton trailer was loaded with 'candies' donated by the American personnel and

was driven through nearby villages and towns to enable a Santa Claus to distribute the goodies to local children.

Work began on 20 December 1943 on railway sidings at Stansted Mountfitchet station, below Castle Hill, to serve the new airfield. The task was carried out by men of the EA Bns., who by 26 January 1944 were laying the rails, although a shortage of labour held up progress for a time. This useful facility was completed on 17 March 1944, but the extent to which the sidings were used is not known.

While still living in 'pup' tents, the EABs devoted time to sponsoring British orphans of the war, and raised considerable sums of money for this worthy cause. In March 1944 the 850th EAB nominated one such orphan known as 'Colleen B' - who was born on 6th October 1935 as seen on this Certificate of Goodwill - to benefit from the War Orphans Fun organised by the 'Stars and Stripes' magazine. What happened to the smiling little girl on the certificate?

The United States Army Special Service Section organised much entertainment 'for the troops'. One of the many bases at which stars of stage, silver screen and radio performed was Stansted, and in the picture right comedian Bob Hope is prominent, entertaining men of the 825th and 850th Engineer Aviation Battalions

Sharing the stage with Bob Hope, and, it seems, entertaining some local children in the crowd, another well-known personality to visit Stansted was Frances Langford.

The 825th EA Bn. began to move out of the TAD site on 1 January 1944, possibly to the domestic accommodation on the airfield site, where the 850th EA Bn. took up residence on 15 March. At much the same time, the 850th's Battalion HQ moved from Bassingbourn Hall to Renfrew Farm, formerly the HQ of the 825th EAB. Prior to this, a complaint had been made by the Clerk of Works on the TAD site, a Englishman employed by the Air Ministry, to a Lt. Nelson of the 850th: *".......please ask your men not to deposit sheets, cartons, and cutlery through the sewage system — they're causing mayhem to the labourers employed in the sewage disposal works!"*

The airfield was dedicated officially on 15 February 1944 by Col. Volmar, and the 850th EAB began tidying up the site. The unit's time in England was almost over, and the men left by road on 15 April for a concentration depot at Cokethorpe, Oxfordshire before making the Channel crossing.

At Stansted, the largest Ninth Air Force base in East Anglia, the facilities were exceptionally extensive. The airfield's three main runways were laid out in the usual triangular arrangement, the main one (which forms the basis of today's runway) sited in a north-east/south-west direction (05/23) being 6000ft (1830m) long. Two others 12/30 and 18/36 were both 4200 feet (1280m.) in length. On the airfield site were four T.2-type hangars, two on the technical area of the west side of the airfield, one on the north side and one on the south. A brick-built control tower type 12779/41 was provided, and there were forty-seven spectacle-type dispersals, an extensive bomb dump with fusing point buildings, a shooting-in butt with associated frying-pan type hardstanding and all the usual range of buildings for technical use. Around the western edge of the airfield was the usual collection of stores, armouries. squadron offices, MT sheds and workshops, mainly in either Nissen or temporary

Those responsible for Chow time! Cooks working for the 850th EAB at Stansted. The gentleman front centre was the oldest man in the USAAF at the time.

brick huts. In the centre of the airfield, Black Boy pond, the only pond in the area containing Norfolk Reeds, was allowed to remain, and this acted as a trap to unwary pilots taking a sort cut across the grass!

Quite separate was the 2nd TAD area, which was located to the east of the airfield itself. Here, Bassingbourn Hall was taken over as the headquarters building and further domestic and technical buildings were erected, including a number of EDD-type storage sheds. Spectacle-type hardstandings were provided for parking aircraft being dealt with by the TAD personnel, but, surprisingly, there was no aircraft hangarage although there were two large, linked aircraft assembly sheds.

Construction on the airfield continued after aircraft moved in. Here a number of B-26's can be seen on the airfield while the steelwork for a T2 hangar is prepared for erection. It is thought that this site is for the hangar near the end of runway 18.

Chapter Two

The USAAF Presence

Although the airfield and facilities were far from complete, the men of the 30th Air Depot Group (ADG) began to arrive at Stansted on 17 August 1943, fresh from training at Stinson Field, San Antonio in Texas. They were accommodated at first in the domestic sites on the west of the airfield until their own barrack huts and mess halls on the 2nd. TAD site could be brought into use. Gradually the unit began to carry out the work planned for it: the major servicing or modification of B-26 medium bombers. To assist in this task, two Mobile Repair & Reclamation Squadrons (MR&RS), the 24th and 25th, arrived. These fully mobile units were provided with heavy equipment and transport to enable them to recover damaged aircraft anywhere in the UK and either to effect sufficient repairs to allow the aircraft to fly elsewhere for proper attention or to load them for road transportation.

Record numbers of B-26s were modified at 2nd. TAD in January, and early in February an additional task carried out was the removal of 'Oboe' equipment from eleven B-17s of the 813th Bomb Squadron, 482nd Bomb Group, based at Alconbury, and possibly from a number of B-24s. The two MR&RSs, however, left in February.

The 'Silver Streaks'

Stansted - now known as Station 169 - really came to life on 9 February 1944, when the first elements of the 344th Bomb Group (BG) of the US 9th Air Force began to arrive from the United States under the command of Col. Reginald F. Vance. Known as the 'Silver Streaks', the Group

comprised four Bomb Squadrons (BS), the 494th, 495th, 496th and 497th, and a Headquarters section, and sported the motto "Win or Die". Domestic areas on the 2nd. TAD site now became available, and the 30th ADG men moved over, releasing their original buildings for use by the 344th BG personnel. On arrival at Stansted, the men in the first party quickly set about the task of receiving the fully-trained combat crews, who were due to fly their B-26 Marauder aircraft in from the United States via Brazil and North Africa. Soon, adequate living accommodation was available in Nissen huts, while in the technical area two buildings were taken over by Operations, Intelligence, Communications and Personnel departments. An officers' Club came into use, while the enlisted men had the use of a consolidated mess hall and an Aero Club sponsored by the Red Cross. A building near the flight line was earmarked for post-mission interrogation and another as a photographic laboratory with the most up-to-date equipment. Other buildings served as rest rooms for crews to use during the inevitable periods of waiting for something to happen or housed the Link trainer and bombing trainer equipment.

The aircraft to equip the 344th BG had, meanwhile, left Morrison Field in the United States on 20 January for Borinquin, Puerto Rico, and thence flew the South Atlantic route, making landfall at RAF St. Mawgan in Cornwall. Their journey took a month, the first aircraft arriving at Stansted on 20 February and the last four days later. One machine, damaged on the ground, was

The ground engineers of the 497th BS, 344th BG, found time to pose in front of B-26G 43-34274 at Stansted.

Left: With the sun reflection of an almost solid undercast, a formation of 344th BG B-26s are snapped en-route to the target.
Below: Home again safely! The tired crew of "Rum Buggy II" pose in front of their B-26: back —
Front: Dave Freedman (tail gunner), Glen Stewart (radio op/gunner), John Dube (engineer/gunner).
Rear: Mike Solas (bombardier), Norman Nelson (pilot), Owen Lansdowne (co-pilot).

left behind at Belem, the crew riding in another aircraft to Stansted.

Training flights to familiarise the crews with landmarks in southern England and to sort out any navigational problems were soon under way. Then, on 29 February 1944, the first diversionary mission was mounted, during which Col. Vance led a formation of B-26s to within two to three miles of the French coast before returning unharmed to Stansted.

The 344th BG went into action on 6 March 1944, when 37 B-26s raided Bernay St. Martin airfield in France. Severe damage was caused to the target, but only minor damage from flak was sustained by the Group's aircraft, and there were no injuries. After this mission, spirits ran high, and men not involved that day besieged those who had been initiated into battle, to congratulate them and to listen to their accounts of the raid. Next day, 36 aircraft raided another enemy airfield in France, Conches, with even greater success, bringing a commendation to the Group from the Commander of the 99th Combat Bombardment Wing (CBW).

Not all aircraft made it back in one piece. Interested enlisted men inspecting the remains of B-26B-50-MA 42-95917 [Y5:J] after its crash-landing at Stansted in 1944. Named "Shopwork Angel", this aircraft belonged to the 495th BS, 344th BG. [Roger A. Freeman]

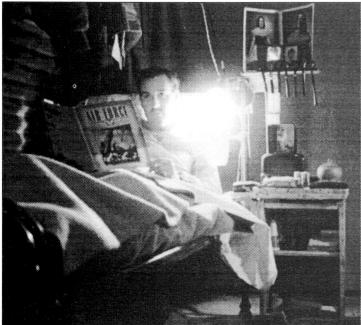

Domestic life at Stansted!

Above: The scene in a Nissen Hut of the 344th Bomb Group as an airman relaxes 'off duty'. He is reading 'Air Force' the forces magazine. On the packing case bedside table is a Bakelite radio, photographs of what appears to be movie stars and a rack of seven pipes - one for each day of the week perhaps?

Above right: Standard on-base transportation was the bicycle. Here Jack Terrill leaves his Nissen hut barrack to go to work.

[Jack A. Terrill]

Right: Off-duty, with the very necessary bicycles at the ready, two airmen stand outside their Nissen hut barracks.

On the third day, 8 March, things were rather different. No less than 54 aircraft took off to raid Soesterberg airfield in Holland, but soon experienced difficulty with the 'join-up' procedure due to bad weather and poor visibility over south-east England. Sadly, the first major accident to 344th BG aircraft and crews then occured, two of the B-26s colliding in mid-air and crashing, with the loss of the complete crews. The remainder of the Group carried on to the target and dropped their bombs successfully without mishap, but there must have been sad faces at Stansted that evening.

After a lull in operations until 19 March due to bad weather over the continent, a change of target type took place. That day, 37 B-26s took off to hit a 'Noball' target — a V.1 launch site — in a wooded area at Bois de Huit Rue. This small target proved difficult to locate, and most bombs fell wide of the target.

During this period, Luftwaffe aircraft were seen overhead most nights on their way to raid targets in eastern England, particularly Chelmsford, from where flashes of exploding bombs could be seen. The Station's anti-aircraft defences blazed away when raiders were caught

THE STANSTED EXPERIENCE

Stansted at war!

Not the best of photographs, but wartime pictures are hard to come by - a B-26 of the 344th BG lifts offf for another mission.

Below: Stansted's control tower, type 12779, soon after construction. On the roof is a Seco 'glasshouse', widely used on US air bases.

in the searchlights, but without any recorded successes.

Railway marshalling yards at Creil and Hirson in northern France were the 344th's targets on 20, 23 and 25 March 1944, with no losses to the Group. The vulnerable 'choke' points of the yards were hit, destroying tracks, wagons and engine sheds. 26 March turned out to be a 'red letter' day in the medium bomber Groups of the 9th Air Force, as heavy losses suffered during an early attack on Ijmuiden by another Group were to be avenged by a raid on submarine pens under construction there. Fifty-two B-26s were despatched by the 344th BG, one of eleven B-26

Groups involved, led by the 322nd. Almost all their bombs were dropped, some scoring direct hits on the concrete roofs of the submarine pens, causing irrepairable damage. Great satisfaction was felt by all concerned at the outcome of this raid, which went some way to boosting morale among those Groups which had taken the brunt of the previous punishment .

Much cheered, the 'Silver Streaks' turned their attention back to the V.1 launch site being built at Bois de Huit on 27 March, although weather conditions were poor. Pathfinder aircraft carrying special navigational equipment led the B-26s, but malfunctions occured, and the Group returned to base with bombs still on board.

Overnight passes for 2nd. TAD men were stopped during most of April, probably in order to maximise the effort being put in, and May was spent mostly in repairing battle-damaged aircraft, of which there were plenty.

Two raids were mounted by the 344th on 10 April, and although the first was not successful the second target, a railway yard at Namur in Belgium, was attacked by 38 aircraft with excellent results. Another marshalling yard, at Montignies, felt the weight of the 344th's bombs

Nissen hut accommodation on Site No.2 at Stansted. Fifteen men lived in each hut. In the background is Colchester Hall.

A view of Stansted, in its original form in April 1944, from a great height. The widely-dispersed domestic sites used by the 344th BG can be seen to the west of the airfield, the 2nd Air Depot area to the north-east and the bomb dump on the south-east side.

next day, but cloud cover prevented accurate damage assessment. This problem hampered 40 'Silver Streaks' on their raid on yards at St. Ghislain on 12 April. The first box of aircraft missed the target, but the second box attacked the secondary target, Middlekirke airfield in Belgium, with some success. Accurate flak caused wounds to three of the Group's airmen, and one severely damaged B-26 crash-landed on English soil, with no injuries to the crew.

After a five-day break, the next target was yet another marshalling yard, one small but significant part of the 9th Air Force's task — softening up occupied France in readiness for the planned invasion of Europe. Excellent results were obtained and the Group's morale soared. Next day, after an abortive mission in the morning, forty B-26s took off to raid a V.1 site at Cocove, dropping bombs accurately on the launching ramps and associated buildings. Eighteen aircraft received flak damage, but all returned safely to base.

Another abortive mission led by pathfinders through bad weather took place on 20 April, but later that day a raid on a V.1 site at Notre Dame

Ferme was highly satisfactory, the Group dropping bombs accurately from high altitude. Flak was heavy, and three of the seven crew of one B-26 which received a direct hit were seen to bale out before the aircraft crashed just south of Gravelines, the first aircraft the Group had lost over enemy territory.

Sadly, the losses of 20 April were not to be the last suffered by the 'Silver Streaks'. Next day, while attacking coastal gun emplacements at Berck-sur-Mer — the secondary target — another B-26 was shot down by intense flak. Five parachutes were seen to open on leaving the doomed aircraft, but one of them caught fire on the way down and another man struck the aircraft as he emerged. These losses, far from affecting the combat crews adversely, served to strengthen their resolve to bring the war to a rapid and victorious ending. This spirit was shown during the remaining days of April, when coastal defences, marshalling yards and V.1 sites were pounded without mercy. One B-26 was lost on the morning of 23 April after being hit by flak, and only three or four of the crew were seen to escape before the aircraft went into a spin and

19

THE STANSTED EXPERIENCE

Taken from the cockpit of a B-26 in the middle of a formation, this photograph depicts the manner - and closeness - of formation flying en route to the target.

exploded before hitting the ground. During the last few days of April the Group flew seven missions, with great success, but two aircraft were shot down by the Dunkirk defence batteries, one of them diving onto the beach. Almost the entire crews of these aircraft were lost, a sad day for the 'Silver Streaks'. Accidents on this side of the Channel also occured from time to time - one unfortunate incident involved a B-26 which crashed at Hallingbury when both engines failed after take-off. An enquiry found that the crew chief had deliberately wired the magnetos to the undercarriage mechanism, so that when the 'gear' was raised the engines cut out!

On the 2nd TAD site, two more mobile units arrived during the spring of 1944, the 41st MR&RS from Langar and the 47th from Aldermaston. However, the 41st stayed only a few days before moving to Snailwell, near Newmarket, to prepare A-20 aircraft for the impending invasion. Other units based at 2nd TAD for short or long periods included the 16th, 40th, 59th and 91st ADGs, supported by several other small specialist units dealing with such activities as supply and security.

May 1944 began with heavy raids by the 344th BG on marshalling yards and other points of concentration, with some attacks on coastal

The scoreboard on the nose of B-26 'Sad Sack' of the 344th BG shows that it has already completed ninety-nine missions. Here the crew prepares for its one hundredth mission from Station 169.

THE USAAF PRESENCE

Bare metal B-26 N3:F of the 344th BG is captured by the camera over the target.

defences. Between 20 and 26 May, with D-Day coming ever closer, the 344th concentrated on airfields in northern France, with varied results. Denain airfield was one target, and the Group Operations Officer joined in by piloting one of the B-26s. Shortly after reaching the French coast, his aircraft developed engine trouble, and he turned round to return to base, but when a short distance out to sea he was attacked by a roving Bf.109. The tail gunner succeeded in shattering the Bf.109's rudder, causing the fighter to dive out of control, the first 'kill' recorded by the 344th BG.

By now, every bridge over the River Seine had been destroyed by the Allied air forces except one on the outskirts of Paris. To complete the paralysis of the enemy communications system, 36 aircraft took off from Stansted on 27 May to take part in raiding this vital point. Defences were very strong, a solid wall of flak being encountered, and 16 aircraft were damaged, but results were "good to excellent". Repairs on the bridge began at once, work which the Group was therefore obliged next day to undo! This time losses were severe, as five of the 36 B-26s were shot down over the target or abandoned after leaving the area, and no less than 31 airmen were posted as Missing In Action.

Orders then began to reach Group headquarters detailing the 'Silver Streaks' part in the imminent invasion. Absolute security was of

paramount importance, and Col. Vance, the CO, revealed the orders only to his deputy, Lt. Col. Robert Witty, lead bombardier Capt. James Parrish, Group navigator Maj. Harry McCool, lead navigator 1st. Lt. Louis Offenberg, Group Intelligence Officer Maj. Herbert M. Mee, and Assistant Intelligence Officer Capt. Irving H. Baum. Planning proceeded, until on 5 June the word arrived that 'D-Day' was set for next day. At once, the task of painting black and white 'invasion' stripes on all the B-26s began, in accordance with an Allied scheme designed to avoid 'friendly' fire.

D-Day - the end of the beginning.
Crews assembled in the briefing room at 02.00 hours on 6 June, and Lt. Col. Witty let them into the secret of what was about to happen. The 344th BG was to have the honour of leading 600 aircraft of the 9th Air Force into action, the Group's targets being three heavy coastal gun batteries on the Cherbourg peninsular. While briefing took place, ground crew men under the command of crew chiefs toiled to ensure that all aircraft were up to standard. Tech. Sgt. John C. Wilder was crew chief of the lead aircraft, named *'Mary Jo'* after the wife of the pilot, Maj. Jens A. Norgaard, who was to be the formation leader. *'Mary Jo'* was to carry a war correspondent from the *Philadelphia Enquirer*, one of three assigned to the Group that day.

21

THE STANSTED EXPERIENCE

On D-Day, 6 June 1944, the Ninth Air Force's lead aircraft was B-26 Mary Jo of the 344th Bomb Group at Stansted. The crew were (left to right) 1st Lt. Louis Offenberg, lead navigator; Capt. James P. Parish, lead bombardier; and Lt. Col. Jens A. Norgaard, lead pilot. [Mrs. J. A. Norgaard via Carl Christ]

After briefing, engines were warmed up, and at 04.12 hours on the morning of 6 June the first aircraft roared into the air. Every twenty seconds, another B-26 followed. No less than 56 B-26s took to the air at Stansted that morning, formating in three boxes of three flights each, each flight comprising six aircraft, with two spares. Each box had been assigned a specific gun battery to attack at 06.09 hours, 21 minutes before the landing-craft were scheduled to reach the beaches. In poor weather, the 344th 'Silver Streaks' arrived at their landmark 30 seconds early. Over the English Channel the huge formation had been compelled to fly at 800 to 1200ft. (250 to 360m.), but when Cherbourg was reached they climbed to 6000ft. (1800m.). The 'Silver Streaks' were over the beaches for about twenty minutes, during which time every assigned target was bombed, after which they flew over Guernsey before setting course for Stansted, where safe landings were made. On the way home, the crews were treated to "*.....a tremendous spectacle of landing barges and warships in the Channel. It was like a glimpse of heaven over England seeing the glorious sun break through the heavy overcast and dreary*

Then as now, vast amounts of aviation fuel had to be moved around. This twenty-wheel articulated fuel bowser is an example of the many types of motor vehicle used by the US Ninth Air Force at Stansted and elsewhere. [R. Mynn]

Fresh-faced USAAF aircrew of the 344th BG pose in front of their B-26 'Hard To Get' for the picture to be sent to the 'folks back home'.

The B-26 carries what must have been a beautifully painted if slightly risqué nose-art of a reclining semi-nude female figure in the style of Antonio Vargas, the famous airbrush artist working for 'Esquire' magazine.

dark clouds that had hung over us all across France". There was of course a price to pay — thirty men were posted as Missing In Action during that all-important mission. Soon afterwards, commendations were received by the Group from 9th Air Force HQ for achieving such good results.

There was hardly time to draw breath before the 344th was off again on the afternoon of D-Day, when 37 aircraft led by Col. Vance and Maj. Hale raided Amiens with fair to good results. Over the next three weeks or so the Group was fully employed, weather permitting, in wiping out road and railway junctions, gun batteries and bridges to make life easier for the advancing ground troops. Sadly, one aircraft was shot down when attacking a crucial choke point at Valognes on 10 June.

While the invasion of Europe was taking place, the men of the 2nd TAD worked fifteen-hour days on damage repairs, but by the end of June the backlog had been cleared. This was the time when the V.1 pilotless aircraft, known as 'buzz-bombs' or 'doodle-bugs', which the 'Silver Streaks' had spent much time and effort on trying to eliminate, began causing mayhem in southern England. Hardly a night went by when one or more of the terrible weapons was seen from Stansted, doing nothing to boost productivity, and several came to earth within a few miles of the base. One exploded over Colchester Hall, close to the airfield, at 20.45 hours on 6 December 1944, damaging a number of living huts, but repairs were finished by Christmas.

July 1944 was occupied in supporting the ground forces in Normandy, disrupting enemy lines of communication, destroying fuel dumps and hitting enemy troops. The Group's 100th mission was mounted on 19 July, with a railway bridge over the River Loire as the target. Bad weather delayed the take-off until 17.40 and three aircraft aborted due to engine trouble, but 34 were able to destroy the bridge and hinder movement of troops and supplies to the battle area. Such was the accuracy of the bombing that the CO of the 99th CBW sent a message of congratulation on "...perhaps the most successful bombing mission that has ever been run in this Command". Morale was boosted again when the Group received a Distinguished Unit Citation for a three-day action between 24 and 26 July, when targets in the St. Lo area of Normandy were accurately struck.

Stubborn resistance in the port of Brest demanded action by the Allied forces, and on 7 August the 344th sent 36 aircraft to bomb two tanker ships carrying cement, at anchor inside the harbour, vessels which could have been scuttled at the mouth of the breakwater to prevent access by Allied shipping. Bombing from high level, the 'Silver Streaks' met heavy flak but succeeded in severely damaging the ships, and the mission was rated as 'good to excellent'. The remainder of the month was spent in harrassing the retreating enemy troops in every way, but one more mission was flown against Brest, this time to attack a heavy anti-aircraft battery at Fort L'Amorique, with devastating results.

Bad weather during September prevented operations on all but fourteen days, six of which

Base Air Depot scenes.
Very shiny metal-finish B-17s are parked in storage around a winding taxi-track at Stansted early in 1945. The storage area was looked after by a detachment from No. 1 Base Air Depot, Burtonwood in Lancashire.

were devoted to return trips to the Brest area to attack the defences. Marshalling yards in northeast France were also raided in preparation for the continuing advance eastward. On 25 September Venlo yards in Holland were the target for 36 of the Group's aircraft, but very heavy defence by Luftwaffe fighters beat the attack off, and three of the 'Silver Streaks' were lost and another sixteen damaged.

The 344th moves out...

While the combat crews had been as busy as the weather would allow, preparations were put in hand for the 344th to leave Stansted to move into liberated France, from where it would be easier to support the rapidly-advancing ground troops. To transport the vast array of equipment and supplies needed by the Group, large numbers of packing cases had to be built - and quickly! On 20

The Headquarters building used by the 30th Air Depot Group. The tree in the foreground is still standing, at the entrance from Molehill Green into the new terminal area.

24

A row of B-17s in storage at Stansted early in 1945 under the watchful eye of an armed GI.

September, an advance truck convoy left Stansted for the south coast, from where LST vessels would carry the troops and equipment across the Channel in comparative safety, and six days later another convoy followed. The Group's final mission from Stansted, on 27 September 1944, was a raid on supply positions at Foret de Parroy, although due to bad weather this raid was aborted. While the last missions were taking place, Douglas C-47 transport aircraft were carrying Group personnel to their new base, Cormeilles-en-Vexin, a former Luftwaffe airfield near Paris. During the 344th. BG's seven months at Stansted, 146 missions had been flown, and 7739.58 tons (7880.3 tonnes) of bombs had been dropped on enemy territory between Brest and Holland.

Now that the last offensive mission had been flown from Stansted, life became considerably quieter, almost all activity being concentrated at

Serried ranks of trucks, one with a winch forward of the 'hood' (bonnet) parked in the 2nd TAD Motor Transport Park.

Part of Stansed as seen from an overflying L-4 'Grasshopper' attached to the 4th Fighter Group at nearby Debden. Over a hundred aircraft can be seen and counted on the original photograph.

the 2nd. TAD on the other side of the airfield. There, the 41st MR&RS arrived on 9 September, but left again on 8 October, while the 47th MR&RS, which had been resident at Stansted for over a year, left shortly afterwards for Beauvais in northern France. Soon, the 30th ADG was alerted for overseas movement, and late September was spent in preparing equipment and supplies, the troops undergoing route marches three times each week to make them accustomed to carrying packs in the field. On 5 October they left Stansted by road and rail for the port of Weymouth, from where they sailed three days later for Normandy to play their part in the occupation of Europe.

Two detachments from Base Air Depot Area (BADA), the enormous organisation at Burtonwood in Lancashire which dealt with a major part of the USAAF's requirements of aircraft and engines, were present at Stansted in the latter days of the war. Detachment K arrived in the autumn of 1944 to look after a large number of B-17s and P-51s which had arrived from the US factories via Burtonwood, where

these shiny new aircraft had been test-flown before being sent to Stansted for storage pending issue to operational squadrons. In addition to the these aircraft, large numbers of other types, including A-20s, B-24s, P-38s, P-47s and P-61 Black Widow night-fighters, were stored on the airfield at this time.

In January 1945 Det. K left, to be replaced on 24 May by Det. N, comprising 196 men who moved in from St. Mawgan in Cornwall. Their task was the disposal of surplus material and supplies, probably including the breaking up of almost-new aircraft. Finally, aircraft destined for further use or disposal elsewhere were flown out of Stansted in one week of concentrated effort, and on 7 August 1945 the Detachment returned to base at Burtonwood. Stansted's runways and taxiways were then tarred and sanded, presumably to preserve them, and large white crosses were painted on the runway ends to indicate closure.

Thus ended two years of use of Stansted airfield by military aircraft, and the beginning of five decades of civilian aviation.

Chapter Three

Early Post War Days

Once the BADA detachment had departed, Station 169's only occupants were the men of a Care & Maintenance party under the command of Maj. Shockley. His orders were to hand over to a designated Royal Air Force officer who would be responsible for the formation of 263 Maintenance Unit (MU), a disposal depot which would process some of the vast amount of equipment which was surplus to requirements now that the war in Europe was over.

The first trickle of RAF men turned up at Stansted on 13 August 1945, and next day Sqn. Ldr. H. G. Belcher arrived to take over the airfield and buildings as RAF Stansted Mountfitchet. At first, officers and men were accommodated in Nissen huts on No.2 Site, pending a more favourable arrangement. Within a couple of days, work began on collecting a great deal of barrack-room equipment which had been scattered all over the area. All the buildings, which were not much more than a year old, were found to be filthy, adding to what promised to be a considerable work-load.

263 MU headquarters was soon set up in Bassingbourn Hall, and new arrivals to staff the unit averaged ten per day. The first WAAFs reported for duty on 25 August, and had to be housed in the old sick quarters while work was begun on converting No.2 Site to proper WAAF accommodation. The lack of a NAAFI was keenly felt by the ever-increasing number of airmen and airwomen, who had little to occupy themselves with when off duty.

During September, barrack equipment from no less than fifteen RAF Stations which were closing down arrived by road and rail at Stansted, and in addition a large amount of safety equipment originally destined for the Far East was received from 13 MU at Henlow. From 3 MU at Milton came five Horsa glider fuselages, but what happened to them is not known. Improvements made to the Station that month included a sergeants' mess which opened in part of what had been the Red Cross Club, the other part being turned into the much-desired NAAFI! By October, over 800 tons of equipment per week were being received, and half a hangar was in use for the storage of beds. Outside, on aircraft hardstandings, was a large quantity of ground equipment. During a particularly busy week in November, 126 railway wagons arrived at Stansted station for unloading by 263 MU personnel.

Other people at Stansted at that time included thirty NCO aircrew who were attached to the Station while employed on agricultural work (a task few of them can have relished) and 400 aircrew cadets who arrived in December from 27 ACHU at Bircham Newton. These men, frustrated in their desire to fly, helped deal with a large backlog of work on the Station for three days before disappearing on leave. Sqn. Ldr. Belcher had left the unit temporarily, but on 4 December returned as a Wg. Cdr. to take up the reins again. One of his first tasks was to take over Station 470, Hitcham, Suffolk, which had been 4 Strategic Air Depot in USAAF days, as a sub-site of Stansted, to relieve the ever-growing pressure on storage space.

After returning from leave on 3 January 1946, the 400 cadets continued to help MU personnel, who were now being depleted by demobilisation, causing problems with continuity of effort. Some assistance came in March, when 400 German prisoners of war arrived and were accommodated in No.4 domestic site. Their general attitude was reasonably good, although in April three were disciplined for breaking out of camp, altering their uniforms and fraternising with women in Bishops Stortford! Official policy was to free them when off duty, but they took advantage of this liberal attitude by roaming adjacent villages in spite of strict orders, and a few were caught and punished. Subsequently, a barbed wire fence was erected.

An embryo airport.

In the autumn of 1946 the first step on Stansted's long journey to becoming a major civil airport was taken. Earlier that year, Dr. Graham Humby, the Managing Director of Grosvenor Square Garages and a plastic surgeon by profession, had decided to expand his company's Elstree-based fleet of light aircraft by acquiring ex-RAF four-engined Halifaxes for long-distance freighting work. The first of these was received at the end of August, whereupon the name of the company's aviation interests was altered to London Aero & Motor Services Ltd. (LAMS). After the loss of the first Halifax in a take-off accident, it was realised that tiny Elstree airfield, with no paved runways, would be unsuitable for Halifax

THE STANSTED EXPERIENCE

Founder of LAMS and one of the first people to see the potential of Stansted Airport was Dr Graham Humby.

operations, and Dr. Humby thereupon began negotiating with the Ministry of Supply for the use of the disused Stansted airfield on a lease basis.

After successful negotiations, LAMS staff began to move to Stansted from Elstree and Southend on 15 December 1946, by which time three blue-liveried Halifaxes were in service. Charter flights began from the new base without delay, although intermediate landings to clear customs had to be made, often at Heathrow. LAMS provided its own emergency services and air traffic control staff under Mr. A. S. Lumsden, while the airport manager, also a member of the LAMS staff, was Wg. Cdr. V. H. Furlong, but the airline itself was run personally by Dr. Humby. Among the early flights carried out by LAMS from Stansted were trips to Belgrade with medical supplies for UNRRA, and many to the continent to collect perishable fruits, the outward leg of such flights often being flown empty. An associated company, Payloads (Charter) Co. Ltd., existed at this time and owned three Halifaxes, but flew no operations under its own name.

Tools and spares of many kinds were in very short supply or non-existent. To overcome this problem, some of the German prisoners of war working at 263 MU 'liberated' such items as hand tools and sold them to LAMS fitters! Without this facility the Halifaxes would not have flown, even with the ministrations of a young LAMS flight engineer, one Freddie Laker!

Early in 1947 a series of charter flights to New Zealand via Iceland and North America began, followed on 23 April by the first world-wide 'tramp' trip. On this flight Halifax VIII G-AIWT carried Dr. Humby as First Officer and Capt. Thiele as pilot, and Dr. Humby was able to come to a long-term agreement at Lydda in Palestine whereby in exchange for servicing of LAMS aircraft there, similar facilities would be provided at Stansted when an Israeli airline began operating. He also set up an associate company at Randfontein in South Africa, LAMS (South Africa) Ltd., and one in Australia, LAMS (Australia) Ltd., before the aircraft returned to Stansted on 5 June laden with seven tons of butter (some reports say it was lard) from Sydney. In New York, reciprocal servicing arrangements were set up with Pan American Airways.

On 5 June, G-AIWR left Stansted for Heathrow to clear customs, but later that day Mr. Stan Mews arrived to establish customs facilities for cargo at Stansted. The first international flight by a civil aircraft direct from Stansted airport was on 6 June 1947, when Halifax G-AHZK took off for Bergamo. LAMS' office in London was closed on 19 June and re-opened at Stansted, and the contract to carry soft fruit from Bergamo and Verona in Italy to Stansted on three daily flights, commenced in May, was continued. One of the Halifaxes on this contract, G-AHZT, was written off at Bergamo on 31 July, but the task carried on, and by the time the contract was completed in

Named 'Port of London', G-AHZO (ex PP239) was a Halifax VIII operated by LAMS between December 1946 and December 1948 and by Skyflight between March and October 1949. [R. Riding via D.Thompson]

With a bomb trolley carrying a tyre standing by, LAMS (Africa)'s Halifax VIII G-AIWR 'Port of Durban', bearing the South African flag on the fin, rests on a hard-standing, probably at Stansted. This aircraft, formerly PP245, crashed on landing at Port Sudan on 25 November 1947 before taking up its allocated registration, ZS-BUL. [R. Riding via D. Thompson]

August 1000 tons of fruit had been moved.

Sqn. Ldr. Bert Edgerley, who joined LAMS in May 1947 after training as a radio officer and navigator at the College of Air Training, recalls those early days. *"LAMS' administrative staff were accommodated in what had been the USAAF base headquarters, while most of the company's aircrews and ground technicians lived in Nissen huts and other assorted buildings. A few married personnel eventually modified and improved their huts for their families, while a few took up caravan-dwelling. A former US canteen became a staff restaurant which was open at all times to satisfy the needs of the air and ground crews. The huts were, to say the least, spartan, with concrete floors, no heating and run-down plumbing. Many of us used what little spare time we had in making our huts more comfortable. Lino, rugs and curtains were obtained from a disused USAAF store, as were tables and chairs. One of the ground engineers who had plumbing experience provided the know-how and tools to enable us to make the toilets and ablutions fit for use. I shared a hut with Freddie Laker (who later founded his own airline). He was a flight engineer, and a very good one too. Together we made improvements to our hut, adding bits and pieces provided by our families and friends".*

Very bad weather in February 1947 held up all activity at 263 MU, but things had improved by April, when more buildings were handed over to LAMS. That month, most of the prisoners of war were posted away for agricultural work, and a severe manpower shortage was again felt. At the end of July it was decreed that all future incoming equipment would go to the sub-site at Hitcham, and when all the remaining PoWs left

on 21 August it became clear that the days of the RAF at Stansted were numbered. On 31 October the unit's headquarters was transferred to Hitcham, leaving Flt. Lt. C. D. Sorrie in charge of what then became a detachment at Stansted.

LAMS' fruit-carrying contract was part of the Italian Government War Reparations scheme. *"The fuselage and pannier of each Halifax",* says Bert Edgerley, *"was jammed full with hundreds of boxes of cherries, weighing 6500 kg. in all. As the aircraft still had their wartime flare chutes in position, aircrews made use of them to discard the stones of cherries they had eaten. I often wonder whether there is a line of cherry trees stretching from northern Italy across Switzerland and France to the Channel coast!".*

Late in the summer of 1947, one Halifax of LAMS, G-AIWK, was sent to Sydney for ad-hoc charter work in Australia and the Far East, but never found much scope, due in part to resistance from local airlines. In December 1947 this aircraft was vandalised at Sydney and declared 'beyond economical repair'.

In September the South African airline Alpha Airways decided to merge its operations with those of LAMS, and used Halton ZS-BTA on its first trip from Stansted to Johannesburg on 17 September. Other work carried out by Alpha comprised ad-hoc passenger and freight charters, using aircraft modified to carry both freight and passengers. Although it was fitted with comfortable seats, the passenger cabin was noisy, and was divided by the aircraft's huge main spar, over which some passengers had to clamber to reach their seats.

For LAMS, September and October 1947 was a slack period, as the Italian cherry season was over and general freight work was difficult to

THE STANSTED EXPERIENCE

With a winged Mercury figure striding the globe on it's tail, Kearsley Airways' Dakota G-AKOZ was of course based at Stansted, although this picture may not have been taken there. In the background can be seen Dragon Rapide G-AGWP of Morton Air Services, and a runway control caravan.

find. One flight undertaken at that time, however, was a very tricky one, involving carrying a ship's propellor to Calcutta, which necessitated much modification to the Halifax's underside.

Although 263 MU was in decline, it was possible to arrange a Battle of Britain service in Bishops Stortford parish church on 21 September 1947, and eight officers and 200 airmen took part, with contingents from the Air Training Corps, the Navy, the British Legion, the RAF Association and the National Fire Service. The band of the British Legion played at the ceremony, which was conducted by the Rev. E. T. Killick MA, while the salute was taken at the Cenotaph by Brig. Gen. C. E. Charlton CB CMG DSO DL.

A second airline began operating at Stansted on 31 October 1947, when Dakota G-AKAR *'Bora'* was delivered to Kearsley Airways, which had been registered on 4 April that year. The founder, Maj. J. W. Kearsley, had bought a Proctor, G-AIEN, in February with the idea of using it for charter work, and had then seen the

possibilities of larger-scale operations. With his wife as co-director, he set about finding work for his airline, and on 1 November 1947 the Dakota flew its first trip, carrying 2500 kg. of medical supplies and aviation spares to Delhi on charter to BOAC. In charge was Capt. H.W.Waltham, and the aircraft was pressed into service for several weeks carrying Hindu refugees from the new country of Pakistan to India, not being seen again at Stansted until early in January 1948!

Meanwhile, LAMS had converted some of its many Halifax aircraft to passenger configuration for charter work, and the first such flight took off from Stansted for Johannesburg on 15 November 1947, the return trip carrying fruit and food parcels from the people of South Africa to their less fortunate British friends. A further flight to Jo'burg left Stansted on 2 December, carrying a cargo of Afghan hounds, each in its own crate secured to the floor of the aircraft. Engine trouble was a feature of this trip, and it was 10 December before the return journey could begin, and by the

'Nile' - otherwise known as the BOAC Lancastrian G-AKPZ, which entered service in May 1948 but was withdrawn in October 1949, is seen here on a foggy day at Stansted. It was usually used on the Heathrow to Johannesburg service.

*World Wide Freight's first pannier-equipped Halifax
G-AJNZ 'Trade Wind'.*

time the Halifax landed at Hurn airport on 13 December (due to bad visibility at Stansted) the total flying time added up to 70 hours 30 minutes. Apricots and satsumas were also carried during November, on six flights per week from Valencia in Spain.

Another operator in the fast-growing cargo market, World Air Freight Ltd., appeared at Stansted in late November 1947, and operated Halifax VIII G-AJNZ, carrying ships' spares from Heathrow to Gibraltar on 24 December, carp from Zagreb to London on 7 January 1948, and oil well equipment to Rutbah Wells in Iraq later in the month. A second Halifax, G-AKGZ, was received on 28 January, but at the end of February the fledgling airline left Stansted for Bovingdon.

Selling off the Air Force.

December 1947 saw the first of several public auctions conducted by 263 MU at Stansted, and on this occasion 1380 tons of material realised the sum of £15,516. As a comment, one officer stated that *".......a large amount of administrative work was thrown on responsible staff by sheer neglect and lack of responsibility of many airmen and their apparent indifference to punishment ".* Not only was there a good deal of neglect, but wholesale 'liberation' (i.e. theft) of goods was commonplace. Aircraft tyres in plenty were stored at 263 MU but many were removed for illegal sale to fledgling airlines. Large numbers of bicycles, furniture and carpets also vanished, particularly at weekends, when security was often lax. However, during January 1948 the job of clearing all the buildings on the Stansted Mountfitchet side of the airfield proceeded, and a second auction of 2441 lots weighing 1500 tons provided £27,384 for the exchequer.

Sqn. Ldr. Edgerley's next flight of any note began on 31 December 1947, carrying 6 tons of machinery and four Afghan hounds to Dar-es-Salaam. *"We were routed via Marseilles, Malta,*

Almaza, Khartoum and Nairobi, but due to magneto problems we were delayed at Marseilles over the New Year, allowing us to have a rip-roaring time there. At Khartoum the pilot made a very heavy landing, damaging the oleo legs of the undercarriage and delaying us there until 16 January, when we took off for Nairobi". Apart from one of the dogs breaking loose, the remainder of the flight was routine.

The end of LAMS

Misfortune began to overtake LAMS when hard-working entrepreneur Dr. Humby was taken ill in the United States, where he had been discussing the possible use of Boeing Stratocruisers by his airline. Suffering from advanced tuberculosis caught from servicemen on board a hospital ship in the Pacific at the end of the war, he felt obliged to resign, and without his leadership the airline began a slide to extinction. The Johannesburg flights concluded at the end of December, although in the pre-Christmas period South Africans had been able to send parcels to the UK on LAMS aircraft for just £1. By February 1948 most of the aircraft were idle, and Alpha Airways ended its association with LAMS. No salaries were paid by LAMS at the end of April, making the staff very disgruntled and prompting an exodus to other airlines. During the last two weeks of May there was an upsurge in activity, every available aircraft being engaged on the collection of apricots and other fruit from Spain in 6000 kg. loads. But early in June the inevitable happened - LAMS ceased trading, with insufficient funds to pay wages and salaries. Six Halifaxes were taken over by Stansted Airport Ltd. on lease and flown in LAMS colours on the fruit charters until in July 1948 a compulsory winding-up order on LAMS was issued, ending its life. Several employees joined an associate company known as Skyflight, which took over three ex-LAMS Halifaxes in August. *"On reflection"*, says Bert Edgerley, *"I believe most of the staff were very sad about LAMS' downfall. The company was a pioneer in specialised air freighting and we all believed that something very big was just over the horizon. If only the company had been better managed and financed!".*

At 263 MU, meanwhile, the third sale of redundant RAF equipment comprised 2640 lots and realised £21,972, while the fourth was of no less than 6000 tons of equipment in 2231 lots which produced £37,727. The final sale, on 17 July 1948, was small in comparison, producing £12,702 for 1135 tons of material.

Kearsley Airways was prospering, and a second Dakota, G-AKDT, was delivered in May 1948. It left Stansted on 30 June for Calcutta carrying a ship's propellor shaft, and, like its partner, was put into service on a time charter basis carrying refugees before returning to Stansted at the end of July. More significant to Europeans was the Berlin Airlift, for which Kearsley's Dakota G-AKDT was sent to Fassberg on 4 August 1948 as one of the first civilian aircraft to take part in this massive operation. Its base was moved to Lubeck on 28 August, and another Dakota, G-AKAR, joined in at the end of September before both moved to Fuhlsbuttel. After flying 246 sorties in 680 hours on the airlift and uplifting 888.6 tones of freight, Kearsley's two aircraft were withdrawn on 10 November 1948 and returned to Stansted. Before leaving for Germany the second aircraft had flown on a 34-day round trip to Borneo and Singapore, arriving at Stansted on 18 September, and had also flown racing pigeons around Europe.

Skyflight was also involved in the airlift, sending its first Halifax to Wunstorf on 11 September, but this airline's participation did not last long, the two aircraft, G-AKBR and G-AIWP, returning to Stansted on 6 October after flying only 40 sorties. After this little bit of excitement, Skyflight employed its aircraft on fruit flights from Orange and Paris to both Stansted and Bovingdon.

During 1948 Stansted was considered for development as London's second main airport, to take overflow traffic from Heathrow mainly in the summer months, as were Gatwick, Blackbushe (Hampshire) and Fairlop, a wartime fighter airfield near Romford. However, the decision went in favour of Gatwick, with Blackbushe as a diversion airport due to its proximity to Heathrow, an advantage which in the end acted against it!

The end of 263 MU's short life was now in sight, and on 1 September 2100 tons of equipment which was considered unsaleable were despatched to the Ministry of Supply and 132 tons to other RAF units. A final scavenge was then made by a local scrap merchant and all buildings were checked. On 1 January 1949, 263 MU, its task completed, officially closed down, and the Royal Air Force left Stansted, never to return except as visitors. Stansted airport was de-requisitioned and officially handed over to the Ministry of Civil Aviation by the Air Ministry on the last day of the month.

Early in January a third Dakota, G-AKOZ *'Mistral'*, joined Kearsley Airways' fleet and went into the hangar for refurbishment. The airline resumed general charter flying after returning from the Berlin airlift, and carried out some IT charters for associated company Kearsley Travel of Regent Street, as well as freight charters for Baltic Exchange, mainly comprising spare parts for ships stranded in foreign ports. Early in February 1949 two of the Dakotas flew seamen from Gibraltar to Bombay and on the return journey brought Indians from Bombay to Tangier. Skyflight, however, was not so lucky, all operations ceasing by the end of May 1949.

Stansted was discussed in the House of Commons on 1 March 1949, when £30,000 was allocated for conversion work in certain airport buildings. The main expenditure would be in installing VHF radio and general reorganisation of the control tower and some remedial work on the runways and perimeter track.

By the autumn of 1949 Kearsley Airways had established a maintenance base at Stansted under the management of Chief Engineer Mr. F.Wykes. Traffic during the Christmas season included many passenger charter flights to European destinations and all three Dakotas were used on 27 December to carry Brentford football supporters to Hull.

The final event of 1949 was the arrival from Gatwick of the Ministry of Civil Aviation Flying Unit, which was destined to remain at Stansted for very many years. It brought a fleet of Avro 19s (the civilian version of the Anson used extensively by the RAF), then Airspeed Consuls, de Havilland Doves, Tiger Moths, a Miles Gemini and a Chipmunk used by the Unit for instrument rating checks, radio aid calibration and air survey work soon increased the activity in the Stansted circuit, which even so must have seemed like a backwater of the aviation world, with Kearsley Airways the only other active operator. During the first few years of civil aviation at Stansted, money had been made and lost, but greater things were expected and hoped for in the coming years.

Chapter Four

The Austerity Years

At the beginning of 1950 the political climate was considered by many people to be deteriorating. In March the Conservative party lost the General Election, and the directors of Kearsley Airways decided to ground the Dakotas for six months but to retain a small staff to maintain them. Mr. Wykes resigned, and was replaced by a man with no interest in operating aircraft, who persuaded the directors to sell them and set up workshops for overhauling aircraft electrical and hydraulic systems. In hindsight, this decision may have been an error of judgement, as within a few months the Korean War had begun and the market price of Dakotas had doubled. Be that as it may, Kearsley Airways, a pioneer in post-war British aviation, had flown its last flight.

For the time being, Stansted was a quiet airfield indeed, only the Ministry of Civil Aviation Flying Unit being present to break the monotony. Black Boy Pond in the centre of the airfield was at last filled in during 1951, a job which took three weeks and involved the dumping of such items as bicycles as well as soil!

The dawn of passenger flying...
In the summer of 1951, however, two airlines began to use Stansted as an operating base. One, Lancashire Aircraft Corporation (LAC), while still based at Bovingdon, started to use Stansted as a terminal for ten ex-BOAC York aircraft.

LAC was the last British commercial user of the Halifax, one of which, G-AGZP, had made an emergency landing at Stansted on 10 April 1951 while inbound to Bovingdon after an engine had become detached, and this aircraft remained there until it was scrapped in March 1953. Possibly more significant was the move from Blackbushe to Stansted made by William Dempster Ltd. that summer. Using two Tudor 5s, one 52-seat and one 60-seat, Dempster flew what was described as a low-fare tourist route to Johannesburg. The single fare was £100, which equates approximately to no less than £1700 in 1997! This was at the time when BOAC charged £175 on their Heathrow to Jo'burg service, which in today's terms would be a little under £3000! In addition, Dempster operated ad-hoc charters to Europe and the Middle East. One Tudor, however, G-AKCC 'President Kruger', was written off at Bovingdon on 26 October 1951 on returning from Castel Benito, leaving G-AKCD to carry on alone. To make matters worse, William Dempster himself was summoned to appear in court in December 1951 on a charge of aiding and abetting Pan African Air Charter, for whom his Company had carried out the Johannesburg flights, to contravene the Civil Aviation Act. However, the Johannesburg trips do not seem to have been curtailed.

Taking advantage of Stansted's relatively

Avro York G-AGOB 'Milford' of BOAC just before delivery to the Lancashire Aircraft Corporation and being based at Stansted...

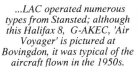

...LAC operated numerous types from Stansted; although this Halifax 8, G-AKEC, 'Air Voyager' is pictured at Bovingdon, it was typical of the aircraft flown in the 1950s.

William Dempster's Tudor V G-AKCD seen at Blackbushe, just before the airline moved to Stansted. [P.H.T. Green Collection]

quiet atmosphere, a number of aircraft on test flights used the airfield during the early 1950s. One of them, the Handley Page HP.88 experimental aircraft (VX330), arrived from Radlett on 6 August 1951 for a series of airspeed calibration flights prior to appearing at the SBAC Show at Farnborough. On 26 August, after being airborne for ten minutes, the HP.88 broke up in the air about 300ft. (90m.) above the runway. The pilot, Duggie Broomfield, abandoned the aircraft but was later found dead, still in his ejection seat. The official report on the accident recorded structural failure due to overstress, but the event had little impact on the design progress of the HP Victor bomber, for which the HP.88 had been testing various features.

In October 1951, a third operator arrived at Stansted — Surrey Flying Services, a subsidiary of Aviation Traders, with directors Freddie Laker (formerly a flight engineer with LAMS, as we have seen) and his wife. At this time, newly-formed Surrey operated two Yorks, G-AMGL and G-AMGM, one of which flew the Company's first commercial flight on 9 October 1951 — 6500kg. of explosives from Paris to Basra and Kuwait. At first, all flights were made from Stansted, but soon a satellite base was established at Southend, Aviation Traders' headquarters. During the same month, two Tudor 5s, G-AKBZ and G-AKCA, were added to the fleet, and in the November, when Surrey took over Fairflight, Tudor 2 G-AGRY and a Lincolnian (civilianised Lincoln), G-ALPF, became part of the fleet,

although the Lincolnian was in store at Thame and was never used. By the end of 1951, Surrey was operating appreciable numbers of freighting trips between Berlin and Hamburg.

Aviation Traders opened a base at Stansted in 1951, occupying hangars 1 and 4. Part of the work carried out was the manufacture in hangar 1 of centre sections of the Bristol 170 Freighter aircraft and conversion of the same aircraft to Mk.32 standard. In addition, a maintenance contract for the aircraft of the MoCA Flying Unit was held.

At the end of 1951, ten HPR.1 Marathon aircraft owned by the Ministry of Supply arrived at Stansted for storage. These four-engined feeder-liners had been evaluated but rejected by BEA, and eventually were converted into navigation trainers for the RAF, with whom they began to enter service early in 1953.

By the early part of 1952, ad-hoc charters, both passenger and freight, to destinations in the Middle East, North Africa and Europe were being flown by William Dempster, and Surrey Flying Services had expanded again by buying two more Yorks, G-AMRI and G-AMRJ. The Yorks were carrying awkward loads such as ships' propellor shafts to any destination in the world at short notice and gaining a reputation for the Company. On 7 June, however, one of the Tudors, G-AKCA, was sent to Canada to join Lome Airways on a lease basis as CF-FCY, and this aircraft, although it returned to Stansted and languished on the airfield for a number of years.

William Dempster's C-47 G-AMSS remained in service with the company until it collapsed. The aircraft then passed to the fledgling Dan-Air Services in lieu of debts. [Dan-Air Staff Assn]

THE AUSTERITY YEARS

In June the Tudors were replaced by Yorks on the continuing Berlin to Hamburg freight service, as loading was difficult on Tudors due to their small doors. Dakota G-AMSR, which joined the airline in May, was added to the German effort in July, but flew under the name of Air Charter. By July, Air Charter was also using the Yorks on trooping and freight flights for the Air Ministry from such RAF airfields as Lyneham and Abingdon. At this time it was decided that Surrey Flying Services' operations would be combined with those of Fairflight under the Air Charter banner, although both companies continued to exist. William Dempster, meanwhile, added Dakota G-AMSS to its fleet in August for use on ad-hoc charters in Europe and ferrying ships' crews to almost any destination. Dempster's Tudor remained in use on long-range passenger and freight charter work.

By September 1952, Air Charter was flying on the 'second Berlin airlift', bringing freight out of West Berlin and taking raw materials into the city. In total, 4000 tonnes of freight had been flown out of Berlin by the Surrey Flying Services part of the organisation by the end of September, and three passenger flights each day were being operated between Berlin and Hamburg on behalf of BEA. Seventy freight flights per week were attained during November, by which time the Surrey fleet of four Yorks, a Tudor, a Dakota was based in Berlin and would be repainted in Air Charter colours by the end of the year.

The 12th anniversary of the Battle of Britain was marked at Stansted by an air display on 13 September 1952 attended by an unrecorded number of the general public. Prominent were twenty F-84G Thunderjet fighters of the USAF's 77th Fighter Squadron, based at Wethersfield, five RCAF F-86 Sabres, probably from North Luffenham, Meteors from nearby RAF North Weald, and a new Canberra from 231 Operational Conversion Unit at RAF Bassingbourn. Among the visiting aircraft was a Dassault Flamant of the French Air Force and a Dragon Rapide from Broxbourne which gave joy-rides.

Skyways moved its complete operating staff and many of its engineers, 200 people in all, to Stansted from Bovingdon in October 1952. Customs facilities, which had been withdrawn due to lack of demand, were then reinstated, and Skyways began one or two trooping flights per day. At the end of November, Skyways purchased the remainder of Eagle Aviation's contract with the Air Ministry to fly cadets to what was then Rhodesia during the next 14 months, together with Eagle's five Yorks, which were added to the existing fleet of 21 aircraft.

The directors of William Dempster Ltd. decided they could no longer afford to operate what had become a failing airline, and at the end of 1952 suspended all operations. The Dakota was transferred to Dan-Air and the Tudor to Aviation Traders, who used it for spare parts required in the rebuilding of Tudors for Air Charter.

York Mk.1 ZS-DGN had an interesting career: originally MW107 of the RAF, it was sold to South Africa as 4999 before being civilianised, and as ZS-DGN was a regular visitor to Stansted. Later it was sold to Trans Mediterranean Airways as OD-ACN.

THE STANSTED EXPERIENCE

The Ministry of Civil Aviation's Flying Unit's Percival Prince G-AMKW...

...and De Havilland Dove G-ALVS formed part of a large fleet of calibration, inspection and Testing machines based at Stansted for many years.

Three new Percival Prince aircraft, G-AMKW, G-AMKX and G-AMKY, arrived in 1952 for the use of the MoCA Flying Unit, whose fleet then became three Princes, five Consuls, five Avro 19s, three Doves, a Chipmunk and a Gemini. The Princes and Doves specialised in calibrating radio aids at MoCA airfields, while the Consuls carried out instrument rating checks on civilian pilots. One of the Ministry of Civil Aviation staff who gave aspiring commercial pilots the night-flying test was 'Jock' Hunter. Yvonne Pope, a qualified pilot, was one who took the test at Stansted. *"As a widow, I had two young sons to support, and found work as a full-time flying instructor at Exeter"* she recalls. *"A commercial flying training school was started there, and it was decided that I should obtain the instrument rating so that we would be able to offer a more complete training syllabus to our students. Having struggled through the Link training I attempted the flying test on the MoCA's Dove at Stansted, never having flown a twin-engined aircraft before! I took the normal six attempts to succeed, and developed a love/hate relationship with Stansted. But I must*

say that Jock Hunter and his colleagues did everything they could to explain my faults. Jock and Betty Hunter's home near the airport became a haven which has lasted to the present day. Nevertheless, I was still scared stiff when I had to fly with Jock as examiner, as his standards were so high".

Slowly but steadily Stansted now began to grow. In January 1953, Scottish Airlines, based at Prestwick, decided to set up an out-station at Stansted, and at the end of the month three of its Yorks, G-AMUL, G-AMUM and G-AMUN, began carrying cadets to Montreal after the aircraft had been modified to 50-seat configuration by Scottish Aviation. In addition, these Yorks were used on civilian charters, including many trans-Atlantic freight runs.

The new year did not begin auspiciously for Skyways, which lost one of its Yorks, G-AHFA, between the Azores and Gander (Newfoundland) on 2 February. The aircraft, on a flight between Stansted and Kingston (Jamaica), was never found, and 39 passengers and six crew members lost their lives. Later that month, Skyways' trooping contract to Rhodesia was cancelled, but

Scottish Airlines York G-ANVO marked as XJ264 for trooping purposes, seen at Stansted in the 1950s. Note that the control tower in the background has a different 'glasshouse' than the one used in later years.

THE AUSTERITY YEARS

The ex-BOAC and Lancashire Aircraft Corporation York G-AGOB, now in the colours of Skyways.

In April it was replaced by an eleven-trip contract to carry troops from Stansted to Nairobi in Kenya, returning via RAF Stations in the Middle East to collect more military personnel.

Air Charter suffered a mishap to its York G-AMUU/XD668 when its undercarriage was retracted too rapidly on take-off from Stansted on 7 June. Next day, while its engines were being removed, the York fell off its trestles!

Possible expansion?

During the summer of 1953 the Ministry of Aviation began to get to grips with the increasing problem of air traffic and passenger termini in the London area, which at the time was served by no less than seven airports. In a Government White Paper issued on 22 July, it was stated that civil flying would cease at Bovingdon and Stansted, while Croydon would be sold. Northolt, used by BOAC and BEA for some time while major construction work was being carried out at Heathrow, presented an ever-growing problem and would be handed back to the RAF. After consideration of a large number of alternative airfields, Gatwick was chosen for development as it alone met most of the criteria. It was seen that an alternative airport would be needed as a 'first reserve', and for this the choice fell on Stansted, but it was made clear that Stansted would cease to be a civil airport as soon as Gatwick became fully operational. It was recorded at the time that *"...like Bovingdon, Stansted is on the wrong side of London for most of the aircraft routes. Furthermore, although it is a good aerodrome and would need relatively little expenditure for use as an alternative it has two further*

substantial disadvantages. Its access by road or rail to London is inferior, travelling time being about one and three quarters to two hours. There is at present a very large amount of military flying from nearby airfields [i.e. Debden, Wethersfield and North Weald] *which severely limits the use which can be made of it by civil aircraft"*. This all had the effect of upsetting the residents of the Gatwick area but pleasing those around Stansted, who lived in hope that flying would one day be restricted to light aircraft. For the next ten years they were not unduly disturbed, but Stansted survived.

Another air display, organised by the Stansted branch of the RAF Association, was held at Stansted in 1953. On 26 September many local people paid 2/- (10p) each to watch a flying display which included Meteors of 601 Squadron RAuxAF from RAF North Weald, Sabres of the RCAF from North Luffenham, a Heron from Hatfield, Chipmunks from 22 Reserve Flying School at Cambridge, four Canberras from 617 Squadron at RAF Binbrook, F-84Gs, a T-33 and an L-5 Sentinel from the USAF at Wethersfield, Meteors from 65 Squadron at RAF Duxford, and a 'mystery' aircraft which crashed on take-off! The static display included a Tudor which was open for inspection, a York and a Dakota, and there was a parachute drop by the 10th Bn. of the Parachute Regt. In the evening there was a dance for which Freddie Wilson's Band provided the music, for an admission fee of 3/- (15p).

By now Air Charter was in need of a replacement for its venerable York aircraft, and the DC-4M, the Hermes and the Tudor were considered. The latter was chosen, and ten

A York in Skyways markings but with RAF roundels, fin-flashes and serials awaits at Stansted for the next load of troops.

Super Trader 4B Zephyr of Air Charter, photographed away from its Stansted base, crashed on Mount Suphan Dag, Turkey, on 23 April 1959.

aircraft were bought 'off the shelf' from Aviation Traders. Work then began at Southend on the necessary modifications. The troublesome pressurisation system was removed, as was the heating equipment, the hydraulic services were moved, and wiring and pneumatics modernised. To lighten the aircraft, minor fittings weighing almost a ton were removed. In the end, an aircraft carrying 42 passengers over stages of 3250 miles (5230km.) was created. It was so different from the Tudor, that Aviation Traders gave it a new name - the Super Trader. Several proving flights were then flown from Stansted to Fayid (Canal Zone) and Nairobi (Kenya), and in September 1953 the type was certificated

A new concept, the 'Crusader' Colonial Coach service, was opened by Skyways on 11 November after a proving flight twelve days earlier. The destination, fourteen-hour flying hours away, was Nicosia in Cyprus, with an intermediate technical stop at Luqa (Malta) after seven-and-a-half hours. No passengers ending their journey at Luqa were allowed to be carried from Stansted. Scheduled every two weeks, the return flight was on offer for a fare of £75, an incredibly high figure when compared to the average wage at the time.

Runway extension.

1953 was the year in which, although unrealised at the time, Stansted airport's future was determined. That September, with the agreement of the British Government, the USAF sent in Detachment 2 of the 7523rd Air Base Sqn. to carry out planning for major improvements costing £15 million. In February 1954 the 803rd EA Bn. under Lt. Col. Robert L. Dice began work on a new 10,000ft. (3050m.) by 200ft. (61m.) runway, a shorter parallel secondary taxiway that could be used as an emergency runway, and a number of hardstandings. The new runway was effectively the original main runway, 05/23, extended to the north-east by 4000ft. (1220m.), widened and strengthened. Behind all this work was the decision that, in the event of hostilities between the NATO countries and those of the Warsaw Pact, Stansted was to become a rotational base for the US Strategic Air Command.

While the construction work was being carried out, the resident civilian airlines continued to ply their trade from Stansted. Air Charter's first Tudor 4, G-AGRG, began long-range proving flights to Fayid (Egypt), El Adem (Libya) and Malta before entering service on the

Above: Devoid of titling, Tudor 5 G-AKBZ had flown with British South American Airways as 'Star Falcon'. It was acquired by Aviation Traders and eventually scrapped at Stansted in July 1959. Below: A view of the scrapyard at Stansted about 1956 shows a DC-4 of Logair, a Tudor and numerous pieces of the Prentices bought by Aviation Traders.

This fine air-to-ground picture, taken in the late 1950s, shows the Nissen hut passenger terminal building (centre foreground). The post-war runway and perimeter track extensions carried out by the USAF are visible, and the control tower (centre left) has been modified, but no other modernisation has taken place. Aircraft are notable by their absence, the only ones visible being a Dove near the terminal bilding, another one outside the MoCA Flying Unit hangar and a Prince parked near the wooded area.

Stansted to Hamburg run on 14 February 1954 carrying 24 passengers and a crew of six under Capt. E. N. Jennings, Air Charter's chief pilot. Meanwhile, Scottish Airlines' Montreal trooping operation ended, to be replaced by trooping flights to Cyprus, Malta and the Middle East. It was while on one of these trips that York G-AMUM/XF285 was written off at Luqa on 12 April. Later in the year, on 22 September, Scottish Airlines lost another York, G-ANRC/XG898, when its port undercarriage collapsed on take-off at Stansted. The aircraft was destroyed by fire when a wing fractured, allowing fuel to escape, but only one of the 45 troops and five crew on board was injured. This event prompted questions about the suitability of the York for trooping work. Air Charter's expansion that year included the inauguration of a 'Colonial Coach' service flown by Yorks between Stansted and Lagos, Nigeria, calling at Idris in Libya. Five more Tudors had now entered service, enabling several of the Yorks to be withdrawn. Remaining Yorks were then used on trooping flights to West Africa and the Canal Zone, as only one Tudor 2, G-AGRY/XF537, was permitted on such flights. Skyways, meanwhile, acquired the first of several pressurised 68-seat Hermes aircraft from BOAC in September 1954 as York replacements, and began using them on trooping flights between Stansted and the Middle East and Far East, and, from December, replacing the Yorks on the Malta/Cyprus flights.

Aviation Traders took Tudors 1 G-AGRG and G-AIYA and 'stretched' them into Tudor 4s in 1955 and the two aircraft then joined Air Charter's Colonial Coach service to Lagos. Other Tudors entered a modification programme to provide them with large freight doors on the port side, with a view to expanding cargo work by the Company. Skyways, meanwhile, began in

Belgian C-47s from Sabena regularly visited Stansted - here OO-AUY is seen on the apron.

THE STANSTED EXPERIENCE

One of the many short-lived airlines that used Stansted was Tradair. Viking G-AIXR stayed with the airline when it was taken over by Channel Airways.

September 1954 to participate in the fledgling IT market by using Hermes aircraft on flights to Treviso on behalf of Travel Planning Ltd.

The well-established Ministry of Civil Aviation Flying Unit disposed of its Avro 19 aircraft in 1954 and bought more Doves to replace them, so that the fleet at the end of the year stood at three Princes, five Consuls, six Doves and a Gemini.

Activities continued much as before during 1955, although fleet replacements by the three main operators were proceeding. Nine more Hermes aircraft replaced Skyways Yorks during the year, while Air Charter obtained C-54B G-ANYB for its Hamburg - Berlin service. In March, the first Tudor freighter conversion, G-ANHI, received its C of A and, with the type name Super Trader, took off for Woomera in Australia on 30 March. Five more Super Traders entered service during 1955. Skyways was awarded the contract in July 1955 to fly 12,000 troops and their families to Cyprus, and began the task on 1 August, flying out via Rome.

One of the ground crew working for Skyways at Stansted during the mid-fifties was Reg Robinson, who had spent eight years in the RAF as an engine fitter, specialising on Rolls-Royce Merlins. On demobilisation, he travelled to Stansted for an interview and was taken on at a wage of three and elevenpence three-farthings (19.98p.) per hour, or about £9-12-0 (£9.60) per week of 48 hours. Overtime was paid at time-and-a-half. *"Working conditions were still primitive"*, says Reg. *"One would be soaking wet outside at times, and fuels, oils, fuel, solvents such as MEK and tricoethylene and hydraulic fluids were handled without benefit of gloves or mask. There were no crew-rooms for hourly-paid workers, and it was not unusual for a 24-hour shift to be worked when there was a panic to make an aircraft ready for service. In 1956 I almost met my doom when a 400-gallon (1800-litre) fuel tank exploded. The empty tank was being removed from the cabin roof of a York aircraft when an unguarded lead-light fell to the floor and smashed, igniting the petrol fumes. I was blown to the front of the aircraft, and came to my senses to find an inferno. With another man I scrambled through the top hatch and ran from the hangar. Of the six workers involved, the fitter next to me was badly burnt and later died, but the rest of us suffered only a few bruises. Under present regulations this accident would be unlikely to occur"*.

There was also a great deal of activity in the Aviation Traders hangar during this period. In July 1955 the Company was awarded a contract to overhaul Sabre F.4 fighter aircraft which had been used by the RAF pending delivery of Hunters and which were now to be returned to the USAF. The first Sabre arrived on 28 July, and over the next two and a half years 99 such aircraft were dealt with. Of these, 79 were returned to the US according to plan while 20 had to be scrapped due to non-availability of engines. At about the same time, Aviation Traders purchased no less than 252 Percival Prentice training aircraft from the RAF following replacement by new Provosts in that service. The intention was to convert the Prentices for civilian use, but in the end only 28 were dealt with and the others were eventually scrapped. Registered G-AOKA to G-AOPY

When Freddie Laker's Aviation Trader's bought all the remaining Prentices from the RAF, Southend and Stansted were littered with airframes awaiting conversion to civil use. Most, unlike G-AOKL, were scrapped instead. [Authors collection]

THE AUSTERITY YEARS

inclusive, the Prentices were flown into both Stansted and Southend from RAF Cosford.

1956 was a quiet year at Stansted, though marked by the departure of the first Sabre to the USAF on 9 February, bearing USAF markings. Also prominent was the arrival on 10 September at Stansted of Air Charter's Supertrader G-AHNO after a round trip to Jacksonville, Florida, and New York carrying ships' crews. A total distance of 4577 miles (7323 km.) was flown, the final sector from Gander (Newfoundland) to Stansted being flown non-stop. Air Charter had by now withdrawn the last of its Yorks and was using Tudors for most of its operations, which consisted mainly of the Government flights to the nuclear test site at Woomera, a two-week round trip. Scottish Airlines, still working on trooping contracts, lost two of their Yorks during the year: G-ANSY/XG929 on 25 February at Luqa in Malta, and G-AMUC/XF284, which swung on take-off from Stansted on 20 April, causing the undercarriage to collapse, leading to the deaths of two passengers and injuries to four. These mishaps left only three aircraft for use on trooping contracts. Stansted's magnificent new runway was handed over to the MoTCA on 30 August by the USAF's 3928th Air Base Group, although it was several months before the US Engineers left for home. During the construction period, the new parallel taxiway was used as the runway and over 66,000 passengers were flown by this means, 44,700 of them in 1956.

Scheduled services carrying livestock, mainly horses, were begun by Skyways from Stansted to Beauvais in northern France in 1957, using York aircraft. During the year, Air Charter ended its Berlin - Hamburg operation. The last two Yorks used by BOAC, G-AGJC and G-AGSO, were flown to Stansted on delivery to Skyways on 22 November, but Scottish Airlines lost another York, G-AMUN/XD667 at Stansted on 23 December. Regular cargo trips to Singapore were now being operated by Skyways out of Heathrow on behalf of BOAC. Over the 1957/58 winter period, Skyways also introduced a scheduled passenger service from Stansted to Nicosia via Malta (Luqa), departing every Tuesday and returning on Thursdays.

Air Charter went through a period of expansion in 1958, using Tudors on flights to Australia (particularly Woomera) and the Far East via Brindisi, and Bristol Freighters on flights carrying racehorses between Stansted or Gatwick this side of the Channel and Caen or Le Bourget on the other. The first of two Britannia aircraft entered service with Air Charter on 12 September and was used on the initial trooping flight to Christmas Island, carrying 124 passengers, on 1 October. Skyways, on the other hand, lost Hermes 4 G-ALDV when it crashed at Measden Green while on a local test flight on 1 April 1958, the crew of three, including Skyways' chief test pilot, Capt. Rayment, and training officer, Capt. West, losing their lives. Early in the year, Scottish Airlines' trooping contracts had come to an end, leaving the York aircraft with very little to do, and by August all had been sold, ending the airline's close connection with Stansted. Finally, at the end of the year, the USAF decided that, after all the effort and money that had been put into the new runway, it did not wish to use it except in the direst emergency. The USAF's loss turned out to be Stansted Airport's gain!

One person who made use of the expanse of concrete was Arthur Ord-Hume, one of the founders of the Popular Flying Association...

"Being non-radio in my Luton Minor G-AFIR, I rang the airport to arrange my arrival. They told me to land, then wait for a 'Follow-Me' van. Now 10,000 feet of concrete for the Minor (which could land in 85 feet) seemed slightly excessive, so I landed across the runway and sat there waiting as instructed. Eventually the van arrived and the driver urgently set of for the distant airport buildings. At 20 knots the van was gaining on me, but at 30 I was holding my own, cruising a comfortable 2 feet up off the runway! As we approached the Tower I could see those in the 'Glasshouse' having hysterics, especially when we approached an intersection and I decided to 'cut the corner' by nipping across the grass!"

THE STANSTED EXPERIENCE

Handley Page Hermes G-ALDP of Silver City Airways at Stansted.

Britavia operated Hermes IV G-ALDI, originally BOAC's Hannibal, from July 1954, including a period of trooping as XJ309. It was scrapped in October 1962.

All the Consul aircraft used for so many years by the MoCA Flying Unit had left by the end of 1958, by which time the Unit was using nine Doves, three Princes and a President, an aircraft similar to the Prince but slightly larger.

In 1959, following the departure of Scottish Airlines, Air Charter, which became a subsidiary of Airwork in January, became virtually the only major user of Stansted when Skyways' remaining scheduled services were transferred to Heathrow in April. Although their days were now numbered, Air Charter's Tudors were still being used quite intensively on trips to Malta, Benghazi and Benina.

The first of the airline's Britannias, G-ANCE, was now being used on the longer routes, as for example when it took off on 5 February with 120 passengers for Adelaide and Sydney, returning via Christmas Island, San Francisco and Montreal to land at Stansted seven days later. The second Britannia joined the fleet in March, heralding the withdrawal of the Tudor fleet. Those used on the Australia service returned to Stansted for the last time in April 1959 and those in the Middle East came home in June, the last one, G-AHNL, landing at Stansted from Lisbon on 16 June as the final Tudor revenue-earning flight by Air Charter. The same aircraft was the last Tudor to fly, arriving from Southend on a positioning flight on

1 November 1959 before being scrapped. Meanwhile, the Britannias were performing well, G-ANCE having flown direct to Stansted from Karachi on 26 June. Air Charter's DC-4 and C-54s began to appear at Stansted on trooping contracts and on a regular service to Australia. Another livery on a different type was seen at Stansted on 10 June 1959 when Skyways sent one of their Constellations from Heathrow for crew training.

So ended a decade of development in aircraft from surplus wartime Halifaxes to modern turbo-prop Britannias. It had also been a decade in which Stansted was provided with much better airfield facilities in the form of a new runway and associated features, but a lack of 'trade' persisted. All the work on Sabres by Aviation Traders had been completed when the last one left on 27 January 1958 and most of the Prentices languished on the airfield. In store were two Air Charter Super Traders, five Skyways Hermes and five BOAC Argonauts, silently demonstrating the obsolescence of piston-powered British commercial aircraft fleets and the poor commercial conditions at the time. On the credit side, BEA was in the process of opening a crew training out-station at Stansted, which would help to bolster the number of aircraft movements in the coming years.

Air Charter's Britannia 307 G-ANCD was eventually taken over by British United Airways.

Chapter Five

Consolidation and Expansion

When the new decade opened on 1 January 1960, Stansted was home to just one airline — Freddie Laker's Air Charter — and to the long-established Ministry of Civil Aviation Flying Unit. All Air Charter's Tudor aircraft had by then been scrapped, and the airline was in the process of upgrading to turbo-prop Britannias. Although Skyways continued to use Stansted as the maintenance base for its five Yorks and four Constellations, both airlines were destined to be swallowed up by others within three years. First to feel the effect of rationalisation was Air Charter, which, on 1 July 1960, became part of the new British United Airways, with Freddie Laker as Managing Director. Air Charter's fleet, two Britannias, four DC-4s and Channel Air Bridge's Bristol Freighters (which operated from Southend), was absorbed to create the BUA fleet, along with the aircraft of Airwork, Hunting Clan and others. British United began at once to operate trooping services around the globe from Stansted, continuing the tradition of Air Charter.

A new arrival at Stansted in 1960 was the Ministry of Aviation Fire Service Training School, which had been operating at Cardiff (Pengam Moors) airport. At Stansted, the unit took over the wartime church on the 2nd. TAD site as a lecture room, and outside it positioned redundant aircraft for use in practice fire drills. These burnt-out airframes sometimes did nothing to boost the confidence of already-nervous passengers as they saw them at the start of their journeys! The FSTS was destined to spend the next twenty-five years at Stansted, becoming very much a part of the scenery.

Although at this time Stansted was regarded as East Anglia's largest white elephant in some circles, Lord Mills, the Paymaster-General, stated in the House of Lords on 20 March 1961 that the airport might eventually increase in importance. *"Its future..."* said Lord Mills *"...is being considered in consultation with airlines. The need for another airport to supplement Heathrow and Gatwick is not likely to come for a few years - in the meantime Stansted will be put into reserve"*. Two lines of thought were current: use Stansted as a third London airport for scheduled services; or use it for freight, training and charter flights. Facilities had developed over the years, and the airport Commandant, John Noyes, was able to state that Air Traffic Control was manned for 16 hours each day, with ILS, a radio beacon and a Met. Office, and full emergency cover was available.

A further new venture was another of Freddie Laker's companies, Aviation Traders Ltd., which

Stansted's Passenger Terminal in the 1960s.

Aviation Traders and Engineering Ltd - ATEL - built aircraft for other manufacturers, as well as conducting aircraft servicing and maintenance, as these pictures show.

Bristol 170 variants, starting top left, then clockwise:Air Turas' Freighter EI-APC. Channel Airways' G-AIFO. Long-nosed 'Wayfarer' G-ANWG of Silver City. Freighter G-APAV in Sabena colours. G-AMSA of BUA.

Carvair VH-INK of Ansett-ANA

Aviaco Carvair EC-AZA

Left: 'Golden Gate Bridge' was the name of British United's Carvair G-ANYB

CONSOLIDATION AND EXPANSION

British European Airways used Stansted considerably for crew training.

Left: Vickers Vanguard 953 G-APEM 'Agamemnon'.

Below: BEA Comet 4B G-ARGM.

transferred the recently-established production line of Carvair aircraft from Southend to Stansted in July 1961. The ATL.98 Carvair, a Douglas DC-4/C-54 Skymaster rebuilt with a hinged nose and raised flight deck to accommodate eight to ten cars and their occupants, was designed to supplement and replace the Bristol Freighter and Wayfarer, which had been in use for several years on the cross-Channel ferry routes, this method of transport then being a viable financial proposition due to the low cost of fuel. The first C-54B for Carvair conversion, G-ANYB, entered the hangar at Southend in October 1960 and took to the air as a Carvair on 21 June 1961. Three DC-4s formerly used by Resort Airlines in the United States were quickly obtained and conversion on a new production line in hangar 1 at Stansted began. The second Carvair, G-ARSD, flew on 25 March 1962 and after nine and a half hours trials obtained a CofA on 2 April, entering service the same day for Channel Air Bridge. Three more Carvairs, one for Aer Lingus and two for Interocean Airways, took to the air in 1962, making six so far. Unfortunately, the third Carvair, G-ARSF, crashed near Rotterdam on 28

December 1962. The Aer Lingus aircraft and another delivered in 1963 were used on car ferry work between Dublin and Liverpool or Bristol until the services ended in 1966.

Skyways continued to fly from Stansted, but two of its Hermes 4 aircraft (G-ALDE and G-ALDL) were leased to Bahama Airways in January 1960 and were joined in October by G-ALDT. The second of these suffered damage while taking off at Nassau, but the other two returned to Stansted early in 1961 for storage before all three were sold to Air Safaris in March.

British European Airways' intention to use Stansted for regular crew training was confirmed in December 1960, when new V.951 Vanguard G-APEE was allocated for crew conversion before the type entered service. By March 1961 BEA training on Comets was being carried out under the control of Capt. 'Tug' Wilson, with the target of turning out 300 Comet pilots per year.

Important news came in March 1961 when KLM announced its intention of originating some of its transatlantic operations at Stansted. About thirty flights between April and September, using DC-8 four-jet aircraft, were planned, and a

A regular visitor to Stansted was Lloyd International's Britannia G-AOVS.

A pair of baggage handlers watch the arrival of the first DC-8 of KLM to arrive at Stansted.

proving flight to New York (Idlewild) took off on 21 March. Several British independent airlines, among them Lloyd International and Cunard Eagle, also appeared on the Stansted scene during the summer of 1961, together averaging six flights per day, not overwhelming but a step in the right direction. For the first time for several years an increase in pure transport movements was being seen, and a scheme to designate Stansted as London's third airport was being taken seriously.

Little flying was now being carried out by Skyways from Stansted, although Skyways Engineering Ltd. was still active there, albeit on component overhaul rather than whole aircraft maintenance. On 1 September 1962 the assets of the core company (Skyways Ltd.) and its £250,000 overdraft were acquired for one pound by a new airline, Euravia (London) Ltd., which had started operations that May and was already short of aircraft. Later in the year, 'Crusader' scheduled services were being operated by

Euravia to Cyprus, Malta and Tunis from Stansted, using Constellation aircraft, but these flights were discontinued in April 1964. Euravia's name was changed on 16 August that year to Britannia Airways, a name which has subsequently come to be recognised as one of the leaders in British charter flight operations, and, more recently, in budget-priced services to several world-wide destinations.

Passenger throughput in the early 1960s was fairly steady: during financial year 1962/63 102,472 passengers were handled, and in 1963/64 the total was 104,724. In 1964/65, however, there was a dramatic drop to 79,254, a bad omen for the airport. Worse was to come!

Training flights at Stansted at this time included those made by newly-built Handley Page Heralds from Radlett, which used the Stansted ILS. Among new regulations introduced on 1 January 1964 was one which laid down that for a given landing weight at any airport, a commercial airliner must be able to touch down

Euravia purchased the ailing Skyways of London in September 1962, inheriting a number of Constellations. One of Euravia's own aircraft, G-ARXE was painted up in full Skyways colours in October 1962 and flew services from Stansted to Cyprus, Malta and Tunis until April 1964. Here G-ARXE is seen at Stansted on 13 September 1963.

G-AMUP of Euravia was withdrawn in August 1965 and scrapped at Luton

Herald D-BEBE of Bavarian Airlines at Stansted after a training flight.

and come to a halt in 60% of the available runway, this was obviously a ruling which did not present any problems at Stansted!

British United's contract for five flights each week to Hong Kong ended in May 1964 and so in October the airline's Stansted base closed down. There were now again no resident airlines at Stansted, but in July Channel Airways had applied for licences to serve fifteen destinations in Europe from both Southend and Stansted and was awaiting a decision from the licencing authority. In addition, Channel had asked for permission to operate from Stansted, Southend, Norwich and Portsmouth to Glasgow, Liverpool, Manchester, Belfast and Dublin, all via East Midlands airport. It would be some time before a decision was made.

Stansted — London's third airport?

In a Government report published on 24 March 1964 it was announced that Stansted was to become London's third airport, at a development cost of £10 million, as Heathrow and Gatwick were both expected to be saturated in terms of runway capacity by the early 1970s. The possibility of monorail or helicopter links with the city was mooted, and Julian Amery MP, the Minister of Aviation, said that construction work could begin in late 1966 or early 1967. A new town would be developed to house airport workers, but not located so close that their home lives would be made intolerable by noise. Stansted would be needed mainly for international short-haul passenger flights but would be available for long-haul services.

The old and the new! Above: British United Airways Britannia G-ARWZ makes ready for another trooping flight at Stansted on 16 August 1963.

Below: Although normally based at Gatwick, BUA VC.10 G-ASIX makes a visit to Stansted for crew training. The VC-10 took over trooping duties from the Britannias.

Hermes G-ALDA of Air Links, which it joined in November 1962 from Air Safaris

Movements handled could be up to 64 per hour but BOAC and BEA stated categorically that they would not use it, being interested in flying from Heathrow only.

Stansted airport officially became London (Stansted) on 1 May 1964, and in July a Committee under the Chairmanship of Mr. G. V. Hole visited the airport. It was now that the local residents realised that the decision made ten years earlier not to develop Stansted was about to be countermanded, and much anger was expressed at a meeting held at Harlow. Proposals put forward involved the demolition of no less than 600 houses and clearance of 9 square miles (23 sq. km.) of wooded area, resulting in an airport 19 square miles (49 sq. km.) in area! The hamlet of Molehill Green would be completely demolished. It was proposed that the main runway would be extended in a north-easterly direction to a length of 18,000 feet (5490m.), and two new east/west runways 13,000 feet (3965m.) long would be built, stretching as far as the disused Great

Dunmow airfield! There was, naturally, a great deal of opposition to these ideas on environmental grounds, particularly to the absurd lengths of the proposed runways, and an action group, the North West Essex & East Hertfordshire Preservation Association, (referred to henceforward in this text as the Preservation Association) was formed to raise funds so that proper representation could be made at a Public Enquiry. Joint Chairmen were John Lukies, a magistrate, and Sir Roger Hawkey, a Takeley businessman.

Barbara Muir, the Chairman of Takeley Parish Council, stated on 26 July that *"...600 families would be displaced* [by the airport development] *and a number of beautiful old houses would be demolished. Two new housing estates* [which] *are almost complete would be either swept away or be on the fringe of the runway. It is a great pity that this planning was ever allowed to take place."* At a protest meeting on 30 July, organised by the Parish Council, it

Vickers V.610 Viking G-AIVF of Air Ferry at Stansted. This was one of the many companies that involved Wg. Cmdr. Hugh Kennard - who had previously been on the board of Silver City Airways since 1953. He established Air Ferry in 1963, but didn't stay for long...

... resigning in October 1964 when it was taken over by the Air Holdings Group. A month later he formed Invicta Airways, one of whose original Vikings was V.614 G-AHOY, delivered in March 1965.

Overseas visitors - right: SAS DC-7 SE-DCB 'Magnus Viking' at Stansted in October 1966.

Below:Canadian Pacific's DC-8 CF-CPI 'Empress of Calgary'.

was decided that *"...we should send everyone we can think of a resolution refusing to accept the airport and urging the Ministry of Aviation to seek alternatives."* A few days later, R. A. Butler, Saffron Walden's MP (Con.), told the protest committee that he thought their case should be presented as strongly as possible. The Chairman of the Committee, Mr. T. Sharrock, said that Takeley would be one of the villages to be bulldozed flat if the new airport was built.

Under Sir Roger Hawkey, the Preservation Association aimed to raise £25,000 as a 'fighting fund' and to use every legal method possible to prevent Stansted's develoment as the third London airport.

Meanwhile...

Seasonal activity at the airport in the summer of 1964 was encouraging, many foreign airlines making use of the facilities for the first time.

Aircraft from Harold Bamberg's British Eagle were regular users of Stansted. The inset snapshot on the right shows G-ARKB in the markings of Cunard Eagle Airways, worn from 1960 to 1962.

Below: Britannia G-AOVT 'Enterprise' was obtained by the airline in 1963. This aircraft later passed to Monarch Airlines of Luton and is preserved with the Duxford Aviation Society.

THE STANSTED EXPERIENCE

DH.114 Heron 2 G-ASVA of Morton Air Services on a visit to Stansted.

Among them were Canadian Pacific, which flew DC-8s in from Calgary, KLM's DC-8s, Capitol Airways, which brought American tourists in from New York and Los Angeles in DC-8s, Scanair DC-7Cs and Braathens S.A.F.E.'s DC-6s from Copenhagen and Oslo. By August BUA was carrying out crew-training at Stansted on its new VC-10 aircraft, and that month an unusual visitor was Varsity 82001 of the Swedish Air Force, which staged through on its way to Little Staughton for attention by Brooklands Aviation.

The final trooping flight by BUA Britannia aircraft left Stansted on 1 October 1964 and next day BUA moved out. This meant that as the summer season had ended no regular movements now took place at Stansted, and on some days there were no transport movements at all. Nevertheless, the Ministry of Aviation invited applications from companies interested in operating the passenger facilities! Shortage of work had a very adverse effect on Aviation Traders, and on 23 July the sacking of 160 of their employees was announced. A company spokesman said *"It is no longer economical to continue operations at Stansted"*

In January 1965 the licence applications made the previous year by Channel Airways were considered, and in the case of all international routes were refused. Two domestic applications were, however, approved - the East Midlands and/or Norwich to Stansted service and the inclusion of Stansted on the existing Norwich - Ipswich - Southend licence. Permission was also given for the use of Stansted in lieu of Southend on cross-channel services.

Yvonne Pope, who had qualified as a commercial pilot at Stansted during the nineteen-fifties, later became an air traffic controller. *"I completed my training in Stansted control tower before being posted to Gatwick"*, she says. *"While there, I often collected a MoCA Dove from Stansted and flew it to Bournemouth (Hurn), where it was used as a 'target' aircraft by trainee radar controllers. Eventually, I became a full-time pilot with Morton Air Services, and later flew with Dan-Air as a First Officer on Comets and as Captain on BAC 1-11s, during which period I visited Stansted many times on crew-training exercises."*

Comet 4Bs and Super VC-10s of BOAC were in evidence at Stansted during 1965 while carrying out crew-training, but probably the most interesting and unusual aircraft to visit Stansted that year arrived on 27 June from Rome; HP-376, a Panamanian-registered Boeing YC-97 owned by Contract Air Transport. After three days on the Stansted apron this aircraft left for Sofia carrying a cargo of sheep. Later in the year, however, Contract Air Transport ceased operating, and the YC-97 was seen no more.

Although only a small concern, Lennard Aviation was welcomed when it moved to the almost-empty wastes of Stansted from Stapleford Tawney in September 1965. A Twin Comanche and an Aztec comprised the Company's fleet, and a Chipmunk joined in August 1966, shortly before the Company changed its name to Skywork in October.

Globemaster 1 'Heracles' HP-367 of Aeronaves de Panama, seen at Stansted on 23 September 1963, when it flew cattle to the Middle East and horses to Singapore. This aircraft, originally USAF 42-65408 and later N8199H, was derelict at Milan (Malpensa) by early 1968.

Swing-tailed DC-7 EC-BBK of Spantax collects another load of cargo.

Of much greater significance was the arrival from Gatwick at the end of November 1965 of Lloyd International Airways' fleet of two Britannias 312s, G-AOVP and G-AOVS, and a DC-4. First on the scene was 'OVS, which carried out test flying on 29 November, and 'OVP arrived from Athens on 1 December. All Lloyd's Far East services were flown from Stansted in 1966, and during that year Lloyd applied for a cargo licence to operate DC-8Fs to Hong Kong via European cities, but was refused permission. Instead, the Britannias were converted in 1967 to cargo configuration, with large freight doors and a paletisation system, and were used on ad-hoc charters to the Far East. A Britannia 317, G-APNA, was leased from Donaldson International in October 1967 for an 18-month period so that Lloyd could operate Donaldson's IT flights from Glasgow.

On the debit side, Canadian Pacific, Capitol Airways and Braathens S.A.F.E. transferred their business to Gatwick owing to the poor facilities then prevailing at Stansted, which meant that the only regular foreign airline using the airport, mainly on Sundays, was KLM. Diversions from Heathrow, however, continued, sometimes providing up to twenty aircraft at a time. Early in the year, Spantax DC-7s were in evidence loading armaments for shipment to Saudi Arabia, a service which attracted some media comment.

Will Stansted be developed?

In October 1965 it was announced by Anthony Crossman MP, the Minister of Housing & Local Government, that a public enquiry would be held to hear objections relating to the choice of Stansted as London's third airport and its effect on local interests. One of the vociferous objectors was the Diocese of Chelmsford, which made a substantial donation to the 'fighting fund' organised by the Preservation Association. The Archdeacon of Colchester, Ven. Aubrey Cleall, said *"We fear that not only will many churches be ruined by vibration but Sunday services will become impossible with the noise"*. By December the sum of £22,000 had been raised for the fund, and allegations that the money had come from landowners and wealthy commuters were denied by Sir Roger Hawkey, who said that the money had come in shillings and sixpences from ordinary people.

At long last, the Public Enquiry on the subject of Stansted's future was convened at Chelmsford on 6 December 1965 under the chairmanship of Mr. G. D. Blake. An unofficial poll conducted in Stansted Mountfitchet that day resulted in 434

Air Scotland was an offshoot of Ace Freighters and operated L.749A Constellation G-ASYF on IT flights from Glasgow for less than two months before going into liquidation! It is seen here at Stansted in July 1966.

Iberia Caravelle Series VIR EC-ARI.

people expressing opposition to the scheme and 244 supporting it. Sir Milner Holland QC, for the Ministry of Aviation, said that the airport would need two 10,000-foot runways, separated by a 6000-foot strip, to allow 64 movements per hour. The earlier report which stated that 600 houses would be demolished was nonsense; the true figure would be 39. Capt. Hunt spoke for National Air Traffic Control Services, saying that it would be important for traffic to and from the new airport to be kept away from Heathrow and Gatwick traffic, and that the NATO base at Wethersfield might have to be closed, although there were plans for large-scale construction there. During the hearing, it transpired that the number of airport workers was likely to be 10,000, but no airlines would be based at Stansted and there would be little maintenance work there. Mr. Peter Boydell QC, for the Preservation Association, made its feelings known in a forceful manner, the Association having gone to considerable lengths to ensure that members had all the appropriate technical information at their fingertips. 240 other objectors also stated their cases. After the enquiry ended on 11 February 1966 Sir Milner Holland

QC remarked that he had never been so badly briefed in his entire career. All concerned then settled down to await the result of the enquiry.

Enter the British Airports Authority
On 4 April 1966 the British Airports Authority (BAA) took over the control of Stansted from the Ministry of Aviation, perhaps to try to increase the incredibly low figure of passengers handled during financial year 1965/66: no more than 3382! An upward trend was established during the following year, with 10,938, and in 1967/68, with 13,978 passengers. A number of aircraft diverted from Heathrow caused a passenger-handling problem, some unfortunate people having to remain on board their aircraft due to lack of space in Stansted's primitive facilities. Furthermore, night-time trooping flights to the Far East added to the difficulties. For this reason, the BAA announced that £100,000 would be spent on a new terminal building to replace the wartime Nissen huts which had been used so far.

March 1966 saw some modernisation to the CAA Flying Unit's fleet. Two Avro 748 turbo-prop aircraft were ordered to replace Doves and Princes and the Unit's first pure-jet aircraft, a

Among other British Eagle machines seen at Stansted was Viscount 701 G-ALWF 'City of Exeter', seen here on the apron on 7 March 1965. This machine was leased from Channel Airways from November 1964 to May 1965. It is now preserved with the airliner collection at Duxford.

British Eagle - along with many other airlines - used Stansted for crew training. Here BAC One-Eleven G-ATPK 'Spur' is seen on such duties.

CONSOLIDATION AND EXPANSION

HS.125, was leased from Gregory Air Taxis as a stop-gap before delivery of a similar aircraft which had been ordered from the manufacturers.

Passenger handling at Stansted was taken over from BAA in May 1966 by Avia, and one immediate effect was the arrival of Luft Transport Union (LTU), which had planned to use Southend as a terminal. Very soon, Friendships of LTU began to appear at Stansted from Dusseldorf on Friday evenings, a welcome increase in traffic. Another German airline, Condor Flugdienst, began operating Viscounts to Stansted twice a week from Dusseldorf but after four weeks became dissatisfied with the handling arrangements and moved to Southend. An unusual visitor on 14 April was Tu.104A CCCP-42456 of Aeroflot, which was diverted from Heathrow with a technical problem which kept it at Stansted for three days. During May C-130 Hercules 402 of the South African Air Force was present for five days. Crew training flights by BAC 1-11s of British Eagle were seen that summer, but at the end of June BOAC switched its training to RAF Wattisham for a time, as Stansted was reported as *"having other commitments"*.

In 1967 the Ford Motor Company, with UK headquarters at Brentwood in Essex, became part of the new Ford of Europe, which was given the task of co-ordinating the various activities carried out by the company in Europe. As part of an overall plan, it was decided to follow the lead set in the USA and establish an Air Transportation Department to provide a secure and flexible service for managers and technicians. Fordair was set up at the nearest major airport to Ford's Brentwood headquarters - Stansted - and Gulfstream I G-ASXT was acquired from Shell Oil. A maintenance contract was arranged with Aviation Traders, and one licenced engineer was taken onto the small staff of Fordair. Accommodation was half of the former Scottish Airways hangar, with a Nissen hut as an office. At 08.05 on 14 August 1967 the Gulfstream took off for Cologne on Fordair's first scheduled service, and soon established a reputation for punctuality.

At much the same time, there was a report in the press that Caledonian and Lloyd International wished to set up a joint engineering base at Stansted, but this proposal came to nothing when the Air Registration Board refused to sanction it on the grounds that no suitable hangarage was available. Lloyd International was still involved in the cargo services to Hong Kong, although as its application for a scheduled service licence had been refused the flights were being carried out on an ad hoc basis.

Development uncertainties
Referring to the perennial subject of London's third airport, Peter Masefield, the Chairman of BAA, said on 6 January 1967 that *"unless a decision is taken soon... ...traffic may have to be turned away to Paris or other airports on the Continent"*. He emphasised that he was not in favour of an airport on Foulness Island or the Goodwin Sands, as they would be too expensive.

Douglas DC-4 G-APEZ of Ace Freighters undergoes maintenance 'in the open' at Stansted.

THE STANSTED EXPERIENCE

Caledonian Airways' DC-7C G-ASML 'County of Ayr' was leased from SABENA from 1963 to 1965. Although normally used on Transatlantic affinity flights from Gatwick, it visited Stansted for the odd trooping flight, as seen here.

"By 1980", he said, *"London's airports will have to cater for 80 million passengers — 30 million at Heathrow, 20 million at Gatwick and 30 million at a third airport."* Meanwhile, Sir Roger Hawkey said that *"...the Ministry of Aviation men at the enquiry had been slaughtered. Stansted had been put up after inadequate assessment."* Three weeks later Sir Roger asked whether in the early 1970s people would want to make a 36-mile (58km.) journey through the East End of London to reach Stansted airport before making a three-hour [sic] flight to New York. A "serious proposal" to close Heathrow and Southend airports and open a large new airport on the Isle of Sheppey in north Kent had been made recently. Next day Peter Masefield replied, stating that Sheppey was not a viable alternative due to its high building costs, its distance from London, poor access and its bad location for air traffic control purposes.

It was 12 May 1967 before the official report on development of Stansted Airport was published in the form of a White Paper - "The Third London Airport" - in which it was stated that Stansted had great advantages over alternative sites for development, namely cost, passenger access, and air traffic control considerations. Although the Inspector agreed that development of Stansted would be *"...a calamity for the neighbourhood"*, he confirmed that work on a new terminal building would go ahead, for completion at the end of 1968, and stated that by 1974 the new airport would be fully operational, with two runways in use. Costs would total £47 million, and the airport would absorb 2500 acres (1012 hectares) of mainly good agricultural land and would give employment to 20,000 people. Peter Jay MP, the President of the Board of Trade, remarked that two additional runways might be built in the 1980s. The Ministry of Aviation conceded that about twenty schools and a hospital would have to close due to excessive noise, which would also affect 7000 homes. A former Essex County councillor, Benjamin Ford MP, was in favour of the development, remarking *"Many people in Essex will welcome the statement, which is long overdue, as providing a new dynamic in the area."* Brig. T. F. Collins, the Chairman of Essex County Council's planning committee,

Airspeed's finest!

Seen at Stansted on 15 January 1964 was BKS Ambassador G-ALZT

Dan-Air's Ambassador G-AMAH.

One of three Ambassadors operated by Autair, the predecessor of Court Line, was G-ALZV, delivered in December 1963.

Shell Aircraft Ltd - part of the Shell Oil Group - under the control of the legendary Douglas Bader obtained a pair of ex-BEA Ambassadors for use as ten-seat corporate aircraft. Here is G-AMAA on the ramp at Stansted.

cautiously opined that *"One feels that this is a panic expedient."*

Resident's protest.
The decision did not appeal to many members of the general public. Mr. John Lukies, the Joint Chairman of the Preservation Association, said *"We shall fight to the very last ditch. We shall have an emergency meeting straight away. Many people will be gravely affected... ...We won the public enquiry by weight of evidence, but it has been ignored."* Similar comments were made by Peter Kirk, MP for Saffron Walden, who remarked that *"This decision will be received with deep resentment and bitterness in my constituency and north-west Essex generally."*

Epping's MP, Stan Newens (Lab.), asked if the President of the Board of Trade was aware of *"...the depths of disgust which will be felt by many residents of west Essex, in particular those who live in Harlow New Town."* Concern was also expressed by sculptor Henry Moore, Lord Butler (Master of Trinity College, Cambridge) and the Country Landowners Association, which said that the Minister of Housing had over-ridden objections and chosen to *"...inflict this calamity over 10,000 acres [4048 hectares] of agricultural land."* *"If the drain of land continued"*, said the statement, *"the effect on food supplies would become critical."* The South-East Economic Planning Council added its voice on 17 May, remarking that the body was

L1049H Constellation CF-WWH of Nordair visited Stansted on 29 June 1966 for the start of a series of charters to and from Belfast, flyingcargoes of cigarettes to get around a British seaman's strike!

Shannon Air's green, white and gold DC-4 EI-ANL, was an occasional visitor, seen here at Stansted on 18 December 1964.

Military visitors were not unusual at Stansted, although some types were!

Above: Armee de l'Air Vautour 602, a very unusual type to visit Stansted, seen on 17 June 1960.

Left: '402', a C-130 of the South African Air Force.

Below: Indian Air Force Constellation BG-583

not consulted about the decision, but the Board of Trade retorted that the SEEPC did not exist at the time of the enquiry! It was also thought that the 'stacking' of aircraft in holding patterns could present problems. Prof. Richards of Southampton University said that an area of 20 square miles around Stansted would be intolerably noisy and 100 square miles could suffer loss of amenity.

A protest meeting was organised by Peter Kirk on 25 May, with Saffron Walden RDC and Dunmow RDC being represented, during which James Wentworth Day, the author, said that *"...constant noise could cause neuroses in children."* A non-political working group was then set up, comprising Peter Kirk, Stan Newens, Brig. T. F. Collins, J. Walker of the National Farmers Union, and Sir Roger Hawkey, who affirmed *"We are going to fight like hell."* Next evening a public meeting at Great Dunmow was attended by 3000 people, who Peter Kirk urged to flood Downing Street with letters of protest.

"Let them know how angry you are and don't be prepared to sit back. If in ten to fifteen years time vertical take-off aircraft are developed the airport will not be needed." Sir John Elliott, a member of BAA, said that he had told the BAA Chairman that in view of the complete reversal of promises made he could not support the use of Stansted as London's third airport.

On 31 May a writ was issued by Essex County Council in an attempt to stop the development of Stansted, following advice by legal counsel that the procedure adopted had been contrary to the natural laws of justice. Protests continued. Even the Vicar of Takeley, Rev. W. H. Branch, joined in by collecting signatures after morning service at his church, which stood just inside the boundary of the proposed development. On 13 June Peter Masefield gave the reasons for BAA's approval of the choice of Stansted. *"Taking into acount all the problems of agricultural land and local disturbance"*, he

DC-8-53 PH-DCH 'Orville Wright' was a KLM aircraft on lease to Viasa when it visited Stansted, and was written off at Amsterdam on 29 June 1968.

said, "Stansted is the most suitable site, and is good from the air traffic control point of view. Those who say concrete is going to cover the whole of Essex are really not talking the facts of life." He went on to say that the land required constituted 0.4% of the county and that Stansted could be made one of the world's most attractive airports by landscaping. However, Stansted Parish Council voted eight to one to send a resolution to the Prime Minister deploring the Government's way of coming to the decision and saying that the Government, after rejecting the Inspector's report, had taken the advice of "some of the faceless wonders from Whitehall who know nothing about airports."

In the face of all this opposition, senior Government ministers remained determined to force the decision through Parliament. Edward Heath MP (Con., Bexley & Sidcup), the leader of the Opposition, in a Shadow Cabinet statement on 15 June, compared opponents of the scheme with "...half the Government back bench,who urged the Government to have second thoughts. We believe", he said, "that the Government should suspend action on Stansted and set up a public enquiry into the whole future pattern of air travel in this country." Lower down the scale of opponents was Doreen Milner, an Essex housewife, who collected signatures on a petition at a shop taken over for the purpose. "Things were slow at first", she reported, "so I went out and shanghaied a few people at a bus stop!" Four hundred protestors went as far as chartering a special train to London on 28 June to allow them to lobby MPs and to confront the President of the Board of Trade, who said that there had already been enough enquiries into Stansted and would not argue the matter.

Although the Ministry of Housing & Local Government asked the High Court to stop the Essex County Council writ being heard, a preliminary hearing took place on 25 June. Two days later the Ministry succeeding in confirming its statutory discretion under Section 14 of the Town & Country Planning Act 1962, allowing it to make a special order and granting planning permission for the Stansted development. Early in July the appeal fund was reopened and a protest

The relative quietness of Stansted meant that it could be used for non-airline purposes. Marconi the electronics group, used Viking G-AHOP ...

whilst Vickers Varsity G-ARFP was used for many years by Smith's Aviation Division.

Dakota G-ALWC of Fairey Air Surveys was based at Stansted for a while.

rally was held at Bishops Stortford.

A television programme, *'Man Alive'*, broadcast on 23 August 1967 on the subject of Stansted, consisted of an enquiry into local opinions about the development. Every person but one interviewed said that development would be 'progress'. Thaxted's vicar gave the opinion that rapid travel around the world might be less important than sacrifices which might have to be made. Although it was generally agreed that further protest was futile, all was not lost. Hundreds of visitors to the Harlow Town Show signed a petition after seeing a display entitled "Crime of Stansted". Every four minutes, a tape-recording of the sound of a jet aircraft flying past at 2000 feet altitude was played, with the recorded comment that by 1975 the citizens of Harlow could expect to hear this sound 64 times per hour during peak periods. An anti-Stansted newsheet, sent to every home in the Harlow UDC area, carried warnings of an 'unbearable stench' of fuel spraying from afterburners over a wide area of countryside, 5000 acres (2024 hectares) of ruined farmland concreted over, and interference to television. Those in favour of development, however, failed to make their presence felt. On 19 September, Peter Cadogan, acting Secretary of the Save Stansted Group, suggested civil disobedience to prevent the development, and on 24 September 300 cars were driven from the Royal Albert Hall carrying posters through the London streets.

At long last the Government began to realise the strength of the protest lobby and on 16 October 1967 the £55 million development order was held up, but an 8000-signature petition in favour of the scheme was presented early in November by the Stansted Area Progress Association. By then, speculation had been voiced about a possible re-think, but MPs were puzzled by the delay. On 8 November the Shadow Cabinet made a strong plea for a further enquiry, following publication by Mr. J. S. Brancker, the Government's own technical adviser, of a statement showing the fallibility of the decision. Next day, however, the Government confirmed that Stansted would definitely be the site of London's third airport, but the planned runways would be realigned to halve the number of people affected by noise! This would add £10 million to the cost, and the order would be completely re-drawn. The existing runway, [reported in the press as being 12,000 feet (3660m.) long but in fact 10,000 feet (3050m.)], would not be used except by light aircraft and would be replaced by a parallel pair of runways, to which a second pair would be added later. The fact that the existing runway was one of the reasons for the original choice of Stansted seemed to have been overlooked. It was still hoped that the new airport could be in use by 1974. In the House of Lords, a debate on 11 December 1967 was opened by Lord Macpherson of Dromochter, who said that he failed to understand why the public enquiry was held if its findings were to be ignored. The Government, however, remained firm. On a television programme entitled 'The Stansted Affair' broadcast on 13 December, Anthony Greenwood MP, the Minister of Housing & Local Government, stated *"If we want to have a third London airport by 1974 we must make a decision"*.

The choice of Stansted as London's third

DC-4 G-ASPM of Invicta Airways visiting from Manston on 17 March 1965

CONSOLIDATION AND EXPANSION

The check-in desk at Stansted Airport on 3 June 1969.

Services shown on the board behind the desk include Channel Airways 'Link City' flights to East Midlands, Liverpool, Leeds-Bradford, Tees-Side, Newcastle, Edinburgh, Aberdeen, the Channel Islands and Malta, while Skyways serviced Cologne. Lloyd International is also in evidence, as are the pair of Servisair desks on the right. Passenger baggage passed out of the terminal via the door on the right of the board.

This picture shows the primitive nature of the Stansted Airport buildings as recently as 1969. Nissen huts built for and used by the 344th Bomb Group in 1943 were still in use, this being the entry into the Terminal for passengers baggage from the aircraft!

A self-service snack bar was provided for passengers' use in the early terminal building.

THE STANSTED EXPERIENCE

airport was confirmed beyond doubt on 15 January 1968. To minimise noise nuisance, the planned runways would be realigned to an orientation nearer to north/south to remove Bishops Stortford, Sawbridgeworth and Harlow from the worst effects. Thaxted would find that instead of being at the centre of the noise 'footprint' it would merely be on the periphery. About 500 acres (202 hectares) of additional land would be acquired, at an extra cost of up to £10 million. This would bring the total airport area to 4470 acres (1809 hectares), comprising 870 acres (352 hectares) of the original airfield, 3100 acres (1255 hectares) originally earmarked and the 500 acres (202 hectares) now added. A further decision was that the new runways should be 7500 feet (2287m.) apart, not 6000 feet (1830m.) as previously stated. Overall costs were estimated to be £45-50 million in the immediate future and £80-90 million by the end of the 1970s.

Peter Masefield, Chairman of BAA, reiterated on 9 February that if Stansted was not ready for use by 1974, traffic now using British airports would turn instead to the Continent. However, Mr. F. A. Sharman, who had been an expert witness at the recent enquiry, disagreed, and strong dissent over the proposals continued. Takeley Parish Council commented on 22 January that if the new plans were carried out the village would be "largely wiped out", as all 73 council-owned houses and an estate of 66 houses built for sale in 1960 would be within the airport boundary. Takeley church would also be demolished. The original proposals were considered bad enough for local residents, but the new ones were seen as far worse. Horace Juniper, the Chairman of Dunmow RDC, who lived at Warish Hall, 1.8 miles (2.9km.) from the existing runway, said that his moated farmhouse would disappear. There was also an outcry from residents who had bought houses in the area in the belief that the existing runway would be used, while a number of experts ridiculed the new runway alignments as being unsuitable for the prevailing wind. In Parliament, the opposition spokesman on aviation matters, Frederick Corfield MP, said that the choice of Stansted would be reviewed by a future Conservative government. He considered that the need for a third London airport had been over-estimated.

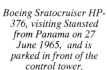

Boeing Sratocruiser HP-376, visiting Stansted from Panama on 27 June 1965, and is parked in front of the control tower.

Sudan Airways Comet 4C ST-AAW.

Development deferred.

Then came a report, sponsored by the Bishops Stortford Season Ticket Holders Association, that an extra £35 million would be required for the construction of a new railway between Kentish Town in London and Stansted. To carry the forecast number of passengers, twenty trains per hour would be needed! British Rail replied that such a railway could not be justified within the first twenty years, if ever. Expenditure of £5 million already earmarked would provide for 2000 passengers per hour between Stansted and Kings Cross, which would meet the anticipated demand until the mid-1980s.

Out of the blue, on 22 February 1968, came salvation for the anxious residents of Stansted's surrounding area. That day in the House of Commons loud cheering arose on both sides when the President of the Board of Trade announced that a new public enquiry would be set up to look again at the whole problem of locating London's third airport and would study all possible sites. Presiding over the enquiry would be Mr. Justice Roskill, an eminent Judge of the High Court. *"The Government has taken this decision"* said Mr. Crossland *"in the light of public anxiety. It is still the Government's view that a third airport will be needed in the mid-1970s"*. In view of this announcement, the Special Develement Order for Stansted would not proceed. On hearing the news Sir Roger Hawkey commented that this about-face was *"...another nail in the Stansted coffin."* Thaxted's vicar, Rev. John Putterill, suggested a day of rejoicing, while the vicar of Takeley said *"This is a wonderful piece of news... ...It gives us all hope that the Government will......pay more attention to public outcry."* Landlord of the Star public house in

Thaxted, Mr. W. Pattison, remarked *"I think the reaction of locals will be 50/50. Quite a few are all for it because it will bring money into the area* [but] *the farmers are against it."*

In a move considered by some to be outside the spirit of the recent decision, work began early in September 1968 on the construction of a terminal building designed by Yorke Rosenberg & Mardall to replace the primitive Nissen huts then still in use. The £198,000 contract was given to local builders J. A. Elliott Ltd., and was due for completion in April the following year. Local residents became worried about this development, but the Chairman of BAA stated on 14 September that there was no truth in the imputation that Stansted was being converted into London's third airport by "back-door methods". He went on to say that during the delay which would occur before a final decision was made in the light of the Roskill Commission's report, Stansted would continue as a small but important piece of the London airport network. The new building had been approved by normal planning consent on 4 April. Nevertheless, the County Councils Association, fearing weakening of planning controls, sought the support of MPs Peter Kirk and Stan Newens.

Early in November 1968, the Government gave approval for night flights at Stansted all year round instead of during summer months only, although BAA stated that there was unlikely to be a significant increase in the number of movements. At the same time, the Ministry of Housing & Local Government granted a Statutory Instrument allowing BAA to carry out major construction projects without planning permission, and BAA promised to consult local authorities before beginning work. A resident of

BEA Argosy G-ASXM rests between crew-training details at Stansted.

The remains of BEA Argosy 'XP which self-destructed on Stansted's main runway, narrowly missing Capt Moody.

Radwinter expressed the opinion that the people of north Essex had fallen into a trap. *"They assumed that the setting-up of the Roskill Commission meant that for a few years, at any rate, they would continue to enjoy rural peace. Already, they have been proved wrong."*

Early in March 1969, the Roskill Commission published a list of four prime sites for London's third airport. Stansted was not included, and Peter Masefield said that its exclusion was *"...a source of strong disappointment."* Many local residents, however, were delighted!

Business as usual at Stansted

Diversions from Heathrow arrived from time to time, as on 6 February 1967, when Comets, Britannias, Convair 440s and others could be seen on the Stansted apron. Although training flights predominated, visiting aircraft included two A-26 Invaders belonging to Occidental Oil arrived during August, N190Y and N400E, both for attention by Field Aircraft Services.

Accidents at Stansted have always been few and far between, but one which occurred on 4

December 1967, luckily without loss of life, was witnessed at close quarters by Capt. Keith Moody of Dan-Air Services, who was undergoing an instrument rating examiners' course. *"Sitting in the cockpit of one of the MoCA's Doves"*, he says, *"I watched as BEA's Argosy G-ASXP began its take-off run with a simulated engine failure as a routine part of a crew-training exercise. Something went desperately wrong, and the 'Whistling Wheelbarrow' slewed off the runway towards us in the Dove, clearing it by about 400 feet, before launching itself into the air once more. It then smacked down hard again and burst into flames, the nose section breaking off and trundling forward from the fire with the crew safely in the cockpit, very shaken but unhurt! My detail was then cancelled, and I went for a cup of coffee in the canteen, where I found the hapless Argosy pilot recovering from his experience"*.

Early in 1968, the BAC 1-11s of Channel Airways, a Southend-based concern, began to use Stansted airport on IT services, as Southend's runway was too short and complaints about

Channel Airways was originally Sqn. Ldr. Jack Jones' East Anglian Flying Services, formed just after WWII with a single Puss Moth. Later, re-named Channel Airways, the company operated numerous types, including this C-47A G-AHCU which they flew from 1962 to 1966.

Channel Airways also operated a number of DH104 Doves, including G-AOBZ, seen here.

CONSOLIDATION AND EXPANSION

Trans Meridian (London) Ltd moved in to Stansted from Cambridge Airport in 1968. Left is their DC-7 G-ATMF. It was not long before they moved on to larger equipment, acquiring CL-44 G-AXAA.

excessive noise created by these aircraft had been received. The 1-11s were joined during the summer by two Tridents, which flew to such holiday destinations as Athens, Barcelona, Djerba (Tunisia), Faro, Gerona, Ibiza, Jerez, Lisbon, Las Palmas, Mahon, Malaga, Naples, Palma, Pula, Rimini, Rome, Split, Titograd, Tunis and Vienna, a comprehensive list indeed! However, only two of the five Trident 1E-140 aircraft obtained by Channel from unsold Hawker Siddeley stocks, appeared in the airline's colours, leaving BAC 1-11s as the only jet aircraft in the Channel fleet. Due to financial difficulties, the Tridents spent much of their time languising on the ground. In addition, Channel began using Viscounts on a service to Jersey, the first domestic scheduled service ever to fly out of Stansted. These services added up to over 100 movements per week, and were the saviour of Stansted, as passenger throughput in financial year 1968/69 increased by many times to 161,926, and in the following year to 224,101. Nevertheless, the airport's main function was still as a training and diversion airfield.

Arrival of Trans Meridian.

Transferring its operations from Cambridge on 3 March 1968 was Trans Meridian Flying Services, the only all-cargo airline in Europe, which at the time was equipped with three DC-7CF cargo aircraft, G-ATMF, G-AVXH and G-AWBI. The latter was soon leased to Turkish Airlines, and 'TMF went to Trans Africa Airways for a short time. On moving to Stansted, the airline altered its name to Trans Meridian (London) Ltd., and Aviation Traders became responsible for maintaining its aircraft. Lloyd International, meanwhile, opened a weekly cargo charter service to Rotterdam, Bangkok and Hong Kong in September 1968. Not to be outdone, Trans Meridian took delivery in December of the first of its Canadair CL-44D-4 transport aircraft, G-AWWB, which entered revenue-earning service in February 1969, its first three months of active life being spent carrying cattle from Great Britain to Ethiopia and cigarettes to Khartoum and bringing back return loads of food products. Another CL-44, G-AXAA, joined Trans Meridian in February, and a third, G-AXUL, in December.

The company was also prolific in the operation of the Vickers Viscount, including this series 701 example, G-AMOJ, under the banner of 'Prop-jet Golden Viscount'

THE STANSTED EXPERIENCE

Channel Airways also flew a number of the larger Viscount series 800 machines, such as G-APPU, seen here awaiting more passengers for the Dutch bulbfield trips flown on behalf of Clarksons Holidays.

Two of the DC-7CFs, on the other hand, had been disposed of in April 1969, leaving just 'TMF in service for the time being. Another aircraft used by Trans Meridian from June 1969 was Dove 6 G-AOFI, which saw service as a company run-about for a year or so. Freight handled at Stansted had increased from 28 tonnes in 1962/63 to 3158 tonnes in 1968/69 and showed every indication of continuing to rise in the foreseeable future.

A company which was to have a long and fruitful relationship with Stansted set up in the original terminal building in April 1968. The newcomer was Servisair, three of whose staff arrived from Manchester after the company was licenced by BAA as its first official handling agent. Servisair's office was in a small wooden hut on the site of the airport's first police station, and from there the three intrepid employees began to handle many of the aircraft and passengers using the airport. One of the three is still employed by Servisair at Stansted today! In those early days, they learnt not to leave the airport in uniform, as some of the local residents who were actively opposed to the airport made

Channel also operated pure-jet equipment, including this BAC 1-11/408EF G-AVGP between June 1967 and May 1968 (top) Trident 1E-140 G-AVYB which arrived early in 1968 (centre) and a number of DH Comets (bottom).

This picture appears to show the entire Comet fleet on the ground at Stansted. The closest, being refuelled and cleaned, is 'PZM, whilst the third back (with a white, dark-tipped tail) is G-APMB.

64

CONSOLIDATION AND EXPANSION

their feelings known.

It seems that air traffic control at Stansted in the late 1960s was not as advanced or efficient as it is today. In August 1968 airline pilots using the airport reported that flying conditions there were becoming dangerous, one pilot stating *"I have had two close shaves recently. Private aircraft appear from nowhere."* The Board of Trade said that several BOAC pilots carrying out crew training at Stansted had been obliged to carry out urgent manoeuvres to avoid other aircraft of which they were not aware. One airline pilot said *"There is no control of airspace and no radar. About nine miles north is Wethersfield. The USAF keeps in touch with Stansted by 'phone. We are told that Stansted has no radar because civil movements are not heavy enough to justify the expense."* In fact, Wethersfield is about 13 miles (21km.) north-east of Stansted, but the principle of this argument remains.

During January 1969, Lloyd International

added Britannia 307F cargo aircraft G-ANCD and 'NCE to its fleet, and then returned the aircraft which had been leased from Donaldson International. Channel Airways continued to expand, and after signing a contract in April to operate IT flights for Lyons Tours between 1970 and 1972 decided that larger jet aircraft would be required. The outcome was a deal made with BEA and Olympic Airways under which Channel would acquire the two airlines' Comet 4B aircraft. Channel also opened, on 20 January, a service entitled 'Scottish Flyer', which involved a Viscount flying five times a week to Liverpool via East Midlands, where it connected with another Viscount from Southend which then left for Leeds, Tees-side, Newcastle, Edinburgh and Aberdeen. This service proved to be unsuccessful, and after a great deal of money had been lost it closed down on 28 November. Nine well-patronised flights each week, mainly at weekends, were being flown by Channel Airways

Britannia G-ANBJ of Britannia Airways is seen on a parking spot at a very misty Stansted.

Channel Airways' and Lloyd International's check-in desks in the new terminal at Stansted, 1969, with four Servisair staff acquainting themselves with the new equipment. Twenty-eight years later, one of these ladies still works for Servisair at Stansted. [Servisair Ltd.]

to the Channel Islands. A licence to operate a scheduled service between Stansted and Dusseldorf was secured in June 1969 but was never used.

During 1969 Air Holdings Ltd. brought several ex-Air Canada V.952 Vanguard aircraft to Stansted and other airports to await resale, and in due course all did find new owners. Typical was CF-TKN, which arrived via Cambridge on 28 March for conversion and eventual sale to Invicta as G-AXNT.

Fordair purchased a second Gulfstream I in April 1969, this time from the parent Ford of America. This doubling of capacity warranted more engineering facilities, and the contract with Aviation Traders came to an end, to be replaced by the addition of two more mechanics to Fordair's own staff.

In April 1969 the last of 21 Carvair conversions produced by Aviation Traders flew from Stansted. As well as those mentioned earlier, British United Air Ferries had bought six,

Aviaco two, Ansett-ANA three and BAF one.

Passenger-handling facilities at Stansted had been years behind the times, but this situation was resolved when the long-awaited new terminal was officially opened on 30 May 1969. To cope with the anticipated continued growth in demand, particularly by Channel Airways' passengers, extensive car parking space was provided. First to use the new facility were, appropriately, passengers on a Channel Airways flight to Jersey on 4 June. Passengers on the 35 aircraft diverted to Stansted on 9 December 1969, mainly from Heathrow, were no doubt thankful to have the use of the new building. One drawback of the new building was that there were no toilet facilities 'airside', a fact which the ground staff of Servisair were obliged to announce over the loudspeakers from time to time!

So ended a decade which had included the low point of activity at Stansted and much talk about whether to develop the airport - the future could only be better!

Chapter Six

Into the Seventies

In January 1970 the first inkling of future development in aircraft capacity appeared at Stansted, when Channel Airways took delivery of Comet 4B G-APYC from BEA and modified it into a 109-seat aircraft. Soon afterward, in April, Lloyd International accepted its first Boeing 707 - a 189-seat model 707-321, G-AYAG. This modern aircraft operated its first charter flight, from Stansted to Karachi and Kuala Lumpur, on 22 April, while Channel's first revenue-earning flight with the Comet took place from East Midlands to Palma on 17 May. During the following week, Channel began flying the weekly service from Stansted to Rimini previously operated by British Eagle, while Lloyd was flying the first of many ad-hoc charters operated that summer to the Far East and North America from Stansted.

The year had started for Trans Meridian (London) Ltd. with all three CL-44s ferrying supplies from Manston to Lagos in Nigeria to alleviate the famine in that country. G-ATMF, Trans Meridian's last DC-7F, left Stansted on 4 February on the way to a new owner, and in May was replaced by a fourth CL-44, G-ATZI. In July, swing-tail Conroy CL-44-O N447T, with a capacity almost double that of the conventional CL-44s, arrived to join the fleet, and by the end of the year was carrying such loads as BAC 1-11 wings from the BAC factory at Wisley to Utica in the United States for Mohawk Airlines. During the year, the Company's name was changed to Transmeridian Air Cargo.

Overseas National Airlines, which in 1970 operated a series of summer charter flights from the United States, expressed some dis-satisfaction

Above: Aerial view of Stansted in 1970, just after the second terminal was built.

Right: Stansted's much modified original control tower.

Part of the Stansted-based Fordair fleet - Gulfstream I G-ASXT. [via P. Kemp]

with Stansted's new terminal building, which the airline claimed was not adequate for its purpose. At its own expense, Overseas National therefore erected a 3000 sq. ft. (280 sq. m.) marquee to cater for any overflow. This event reached the ears of BAA, which said that if more space was needed, planning permission would be sought from Essex County Council. Other long-haul airlines using Stansted airport in 1970 were Saturn Airways, TWA and American Flyers.

Fordair was also set for expansion when in 1970 a new HS-125-400, G-AYFM, was purchased for use on executive flights, leaving the two Gulfstreams to concentrate on the scheduled services. Fourteen pilots were now employed by Fordair, and all maintenance was carried out 'in house', major overhauls having been transferred from Marshall of Cambridge. That year, Fordair made 2143 flights, mainly between Stansted and Cologne. In October 1972, a weekly service to Bordeaux was opened in connection with a new Ford factory there. To alleviate aircraft shortages, Fordair chartered Avro 748 aircraft from Skyways when necessary.

On 16 July 1970, dockers began a national strike for higher wages, again paralysing the movement of cargo by sea for several weeks. Many additional cargo flights flew in and out of Stansted during the strike period, involving, among others, Hercules aircraft of Alaska Airlines and Pacific Western; C-46s of Fred Olsen; DC-6As, Convair 440s and DC-9s of Martinair; Dakotas of Stellar Freight and

Fairflight; DC-4s and DC-7Fs of Aer Turas; and Comet 4Bs, Tridents and BAC 1-11s of Channel Airways, which were pressed into service to carry tobacco to Belfast and general freight to Jersey.

Channel Airways announced in September 1970 that application had been made to the appropriate United States and Canadian bodies for permission to operate 'affinity charter' flights from Stansted, but nothing came of this plan. Lloyd, meanwhile, made it known that it would begin a scheduled service between Stansted and other major airports in Europe to San Jose, Costa Rica, in conjunction with LACSA. By the end of the year, one of Lloyds' remaining Britannias was on charter to El Al for six months and others were on lease to BEA for scheduled freight work out of Heathrow.

More talk of expansion

Worries that BAA intended to expand Stansted airport to the size of Gatwick were behind a protest by Essex County Council in October 1970. Plans to increase the size of the terminal building from 31,000 sq. ft. to 44,000 sq. ft. (2881 sq. m. to 4089 sq. m.) had been announced by BAA, which said that it held a general development order covering such a project. In response, Essex County Council said that it would ask the Ministry of Housing & Local Government for direction in the hope of forcing BAA, which in the opinion of the Council seemed to be expanding Stansted by 'back door' methods, to submit a specific application. BAA

Dock strike-breaking C-46 Commando LN-FOP of Fred Olsen.

Sterling Airways DC-6B OY-BAT landing on Stansted's runway 23. The mobile home park in the background was on the site of the today's terminal complex. [via P. Kemp]

Super Caravelle model 10B3 OY-STF of Sterling Airways.

responded by stating *"All we are doing is providing covered accommodation for people coming into London."* At the end of December, a writ was issued against BAA by six members of the Preservation Association in an effort to stop night flights.

Sterling Airways was a regular user of Stansted during this period, operating a Caravelle on Tuesday flights to Copenhagen and Sundays to Le Bourget, and a DC-6B service from Billund.

Stansted's major aircraft maintenance concern, Aviation Traders, was now beginning to deal with Boeing 707s, probably the first of which to arrive for attention being a British Midland Airways aircraft on 27 April. Other types routinely dealt with during the year were Britannias, Vanguards and the CL-44s of Transmeridian.

Becoming busier...

Passenger throughput in 1970 increased by 119.2% over 1969 to reach 519,534. Aircraft movements rose by 4.9% to 44,566, of which 6249 were transport flights, although training flights, numbering 27,291, fell by 1.9%.

1971's activities at Stansted opened with planned expansion of services by the two resident airlines. Channel wanted to operate jet services to Belfast, Newcastle and Glasgow, and the first two destinations were approved by the authorities, but neither came to fruition. This airline was 'feeling the pinch' and only had one Comet, G-ARDI, in service at the time. Lloyd added another Boeing 707, G-AYRZ, to the fleet in February, and both the Boeings were then put into service on affinity group charter flights to North American destinations from Stansted and Prestwick. A Britannia, meanwhile, was in use on IT flights out of Bristol and Cardiff for Clarkson's, the holiday company which was now rapidly heading towards the peak of its growth.

Transmeridian, meanwhile, formulated plans to operate scheduled services between Stansted and Basle, Geneva, Milan and Marseilles, using three CL-44 aircraft converted to carry 36

Avro 748 G-AVXI of CAFU, with Dove G-ANUU in the background.

Boeing 747 G-AWNE of BOAC soon followed G-AWNB into Stansted for crew training, although it is seen here in the Heathrow maintenance area.

passengers, 12 cars and 10 tons of freight. Modified schemes included the use of 175-seat CL-44D4s for IT work and 100-seat configuration for 'air cruising' to exotic locations in the Far East, the Caribbean and Africa. None of these ideas was fully developed, but three extra CL-44D4 aircraft were delivered by the end of the year. One event which did take place, in October, was the purchase by Transmeridian's Mr. T. D. Keegan of Southend-based British Air Ferries, which without delay submitted an application to fly weekly cargo trips to Rhodesia. To deal with the growing amount of freight handled at Stansted, a new dedicated cargo area came into use on the eastern side of the airfield early in 1971.

History was made on 8 February 1971, when the first example of the Boeing 747 wide-bodied aircraft appeared at Stansted in the shape of BOAC's G-AWNB to carry out a crew training detail. It was soon followed by others in the fleet. Another unusual visitor was one of the United Arab Republic Air Force's C-130 Hercules aircraft, which put in an appearance on 25 March.

A third passenger airline became resident at Stansted in May 1971, when Air International was formed by Captain J. Malanowicz, and in July the new company took delivery of Viscount 702 G-APPX from Field Aircraft Services. This aircraft went into service on 4 September with IT charters to Frankfurt and Vienna on behalf of Arrow Travel. Regular visitors during May were chartered DC-8s of Universal Airlines, which had recently taken over American Flyers' Airline.

Since the opening of the new terminal, the original Nissen hut had been relegated to use as a delayed-departure lounge. There, meals were provided to passengers by Airport Catering Services Ltd., who charged the airlines 52$\frac{1}{2}$ pence for a hot breakfast, 30 pence for a cold one, and £1.05 or £1.10 for a lunch or dinner!

During the summer of 1971, spare parts for Channel Airways' Tridents and Comets (of which five were now in use) were not available to the company, and to overcome part of the problem one of Mexicana's redundant Comets was purchased for cannibalisation. The two Tridents were sold to BEA in the late summer. A heavy summer programme compelled Channel to lease aircraft from other airlines; Lloyd International, Britannia Airways, BUA and even Spantax obliged, the latter providing a Coronado. To cope with additional traffic, work began on extensions to the terminal building to provide a further 13,500 sq.ft. (1255 sq.m.) capacity. There were many visits by DC-8s of Saturn and Universal

Air Internatinal V.702 Viscount G-APPX [M. Russell]

*Civilian
'Fat Alberts'
at Stansted!*

*Left: Pacific Western's
L.382G Hercules CF-PWO.*

*A Southern Air Transport
Lockheed L.100-382E, possibly
N7951R .*

Airways that summer, and Saturn also sent in L.100 (civilian Hercules) aircraft on cargo trips. Other interesting visitors included, in October 1971, two Saudi Air Force Dakotas.

Lloyd International's regular freight flights to Hong Kong from Stansted were increased in frequency to three per fortnight in June 1971, thus occupying two aircraft for most of the time. In December, a third Boeing 707, G-AZJM, was added to Lloyd's fleet, enabling the four Britannias to be used on the more mundane operations. Three of them were needed for the ever-growing Hong Kong freight service when early in 1972 the frequency was increased to eight per month, while the fourth was in use on the Clarkson IT flights from Cardiff and Bristol.

Bad news for Stansted

1972 was, however, a very bad year for Stansted-based airlines. First came the announcement on 25 January of Channel Airways' decision to close its Stansted maintenance base at the end of that month and to withdraw services to the Channel Islands. On 1 February a Receiver was appointed

to Channel, and two weeks later all Comet and BAC 1-11 services closed down. Viscount flights from Southampton to Rotterdam and Ostend and to the Channel Islands continued until on 29 February the Company ceased operations, after which its licence to fly to the Channel Islands was transferred to British Midland Airways, although no such flights were made during 1972. Then, on 16 June, Lloyd International's parent Company, Lloyd Aviation Holdings Ltd., also called in the Receiver, as the airline's North American charter operations were not profitable and could no longer be subsidised by the other operations. All flying ended that day apart from the return of aircraft to Stansted. One American family booked to go home on a Lloyd flight on 10 July and unaware of the airline's demise had to sleep on the floor of the airport police station.

Air International, meanwhile, had hoped to purchase a Boeing 707 for affinity group charter flights across the Atlantic, but this project came to nothing. The airline's summer season therefore consisted mainly of flights from Stansted and Gatwick to Germany and Austria, but in

*British Air Ferries
Carvair G-AOFW was
named 'Big John'.*

British Caledonian's Boeing 707-349C G-AWWD landing at Stansted on 4 May 1973
[T. Harding]

November the Viscount was impounded at Gatwick due to non-payment of landing fees, and no further trips were flown. British Air Ferries were also unlucky, as their Stansted to Ostend car ferry service, opened in May 1972, had to be closed at the end of June due to a shortage of customers.

A fatal accident, very rare at or near Stansted, took place on 5 January 1972, when Aztec 250E G-AZIF of Air London, flying from Gatwick to Stansted at night and approaching runway 23, came down near the B1053 road between Thaxted and Great Sampford, all three on board losing their lives.

September 1972 was the time of the 'rescue' charter flights of refugees from Uganda, where President Idi Amin was making himself unpopular. The first flight was a Boeing 707 of Donaldson which arrived on 19 September, chartered by East African Airways. Further refugee flights were made into Stansted by aircraft of British Caledonian and BOAC. Channel Airways' former building (later Airways House) was converted into a reception area with medical facilities and refreshments, a service used by over eighteen thousand refugees who arrived over a period of several days.

The activities of foreign airlines were maintained fairly well in 1972, regular visitors being the DC-9s of Finnair, JAT and Itavia, Boeing 727s of TAP and the Boeing 737s, F-27 Friendships and F-28 Fellowships of Braathens. Also seen were DC-8 aircraft of Saturn Airways and Universal Airways until the latter closed down in May. Nevertheless, the number of aircraft movements at Stansted in 1972 were nearly 20% less than previous year, which was bad news for all concerned. BAA, however, forecast that by 1980 passenger throughput would be 3,500,000 per year, about seven times the 1972 figure. It was hoped that increased landing fees for crew training flights would persuade operators to carry out this function at Prestwick in Scotland instead and that the resulting shortfall in aircraft movements could be made up by many more IT flights.

The effect of the failed airlines on Aviation Traders' business was considerable, as the company had been responsible for maintaining the Lloyd International fleet and would have dealt with Channel Airways' Comets had that airline remained solvent. As a result of the down-turn in work, Aviation Traders was obliged to make half its staff redundant.

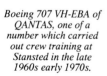

Boeing 707 VH-EBA of QANTAS, one of a number which carried out crew training at Stansted in the late 1960s early 1970s.

INTO THE SEVENTIES

The Finnish charter airline Kar-Air was a regular visitor into Stansted with both their DC6 OH-KDC (left) and Convair 440 Metropolitan OH-VKN (below)

No decision yet

In the House of Commons on 7 August 1972, David Steel MP (Lib., Roxburgh, Selkirk and Peebles) asked the Secretary of State for Trade and Industry for a statement on the long-term future of Stansted airport. Mr. Onslow, the Under-Secretary, replied *"When Maplin airport becomes operational, we see the possibility of closing Stansted as a public transport airport and perhaps dispensing with it altogether."* David Steel then asked how long it was likely to be before a decision was reached, to which Mr. Onslow replied *"...we expect Maplin to become operational in 1980. In the meantime, we are asking BAA and CAA to see what possibilities there are for the deployment of workers to Stansted with a view to their ultimate transfer to Maplin."* Presumably, the Under-Secretary was referring to newly-recruited workers. Norman Tebbitt MP (Con., Epping) commented *"What he says will cause considerable gloom in and around my constituency...",* to which Mr. Onslow replied *"It will not cause gloom to know*

we want to keep people at Stansted for the time when they are needed at Maplin."

Better news was received on 26 September 1972, when the CAA approved Laker Airways' application for a licence to operate a service to New York from Stansted rather than Gatwick. The one-way fare was to be £32.50 in summer and £37.50 in winter. Freddie Laker was disappointed, but is said to have remarked that Stansted was ten minutes nearer New York! Eleven return flights per week in summer were planned and seven in winter, using two 345-seat DC-10s and two 158-seat Boeing 707s. Work began on building check-in faclities for an anticipated inaugural flight on 1 April 1973, and a Skytel hotel to cater for Laker customers was also mooted.

Over the Christmas period in 1972 a number of minor crises were dealt with at Stansted. On 21 December about a hundred passengers were stranded there when their charter flight to New York was declared illegal. The BAA duty officer stated that the charterer seemed to have

Donaldson Cargo Boeing 707-321 G-BAEL at Stansted on 10 June 1974. [T. Harding]

THE STANSTED EXPERIENCE

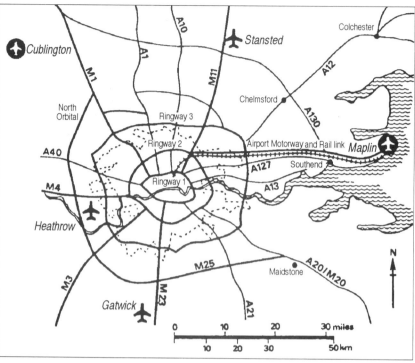

What might have been - the south-east corner of England, showing the development of road, rail and airport facilities to take into account the building of Maplin.

disappeared, and arrangements were made by handling agents Servisair to accommodate the passengers in London hotels. Next day, a number of passengers staged a sit-in when their British Midland Airways charter to New York was cancelled just before take-off due to alleged discrepancies between the passenger list and the names of the people presenting themselves for the flight.

Aviation Traders was able to re-open Hangar One (which had housed the Carvair production line) in January 1973 for aircraft overhauls, the first to be dealt with being HS.748 Ser.2 G-ATMJ, recently acquired by the Civil Aviation Flying Unit.

Expansion plans by Air International, which had not flown since the previous November, were mooted early in 1973, when the proposal to buy two BAC 1-11s was announced. However, they were not delivered, and after planning for local travel agents a series of IT flights from Southend which never took to the air, on 11 June 1973 Air

Invicta International Airlines Boeing 707-023B G-BCBA on 9 November 1974. [T. Harding]

INTO THE SEVENTIES

It was not all heavy metal and fast jets at Stansted. Here Britten Norman BN.2A Islander G-AXRN of Humber Airways is seen arriving at at Stansted on 5 April 1974. [T. Harding]

International followed several other Stansted-based airlines which had gone into liquidation.

Air Holdings was again in the position of having unwanted aircraft on its hands when on 16 January 1973 Invicta International went into receivership. The Group therefore launched its own airline, reviving the classic name of Silver City Airways, to fly both passenger and frieght charters from Stansted and Luton. Vanguard 952F G-AYLD was taken over on 10 February 1973 and in the following month the airline opened an office at Stansted. At the end of March a further Vanguard 952, G-AYFN, arrived, but it was never placed in service before being sold to a revived Invicta two weeks later. G-AYLD, meanwhile, was busy in Europe, mainly carrying cattle from Hamburg and Norwich to Italy. Silver

City's enterprise was short-lived, however, ending on 2 November 1973, the Vanguard being sold in France.

Fordair was still expanding, the aircraft being supplemented by the arrival on 20 May 1973 of Gulfstream II N327K, on dry lease from Ford of America. This newcomer was used initially for executive flights but in 1974 began the new Stansted - Cologne - Valencia service. However, in February 1975 N327K was returned to Detroit to be sold, and one of the Gulfstream Is took over the Valencia service, taking three-and-a-half hours instead of two! A third G-I, N307K, arrived at Stansted on 26 February as a replacement for the more modern G-II, staying with Fordair until February 1977.

The licence transferred from the defunct Channel Airways to British Midland was now being used for weekend flights to the Channel Islands, but the only resident airline at this time was Transmeridian. Overseas airlines accounted for most of the transport movements during the year, many of them using Boeing 707s, which by then were becoming a more common sight at

Above left: Exeter-based South West Aviation's specially equipped Skyvan G-AWCS calls in to collect horses.

Left: Nord 262 F-BLKA

Right: The former Canadian Vanguard CF-TKJ was obtained by Air Holdings and leased during 1970 as PK-ICC to Indonesian Angkasa Civil Air Transport. The aircraft is seen here being returned to Invicta International.

In an early colourscheme and registered N447T, Transmeridian Air Cargo's Conroy conversion of the Canadair CL-44 was named 'Skymonster'. [via Simon Peters]

Stansted, and in Aviation Traders' hangar.

As part of a programme of attracting more airline customers to Stansted, improvements carried out in 1973 included the strengthening of the main apron area and provision of floodlighting, while handling agents Servisair took possession of a set of steps for Boeing 747s and a tug powerful enough to tow the new generation of wide-bodied aircraft which would, it was hoped, soon use Stansted. The traffic figures for the year had, however, continued to decline, and showed a drop of 10% since the previous year.

In its annual report, published on 4 September 1973, BAA remained open-minded on the subject of the proposed Maplin airport. Nigel Foulkes, the BAA Chairman, warned of formidable difficulties at the other London airports if the Maplin project was not completed. Without Maplin, he asked in the report, what would Heathrow and Gatwick be like in the 1980s? Would Stansted emerge as the third London airport after all? If the Maplin project was cancelled, and as soon as Heathrow and Gatwick reached the limits of runway capacity and space, Stansted would have to begin accepting any further increase in movements.

Among the more interesting visitors to Stansted in 1973 were a Transall aircraft of the Luftwaffe, 50+38, on 10 January; Noratlas 9XR-KH on 20 February; the DC-8 of the President of Mexico, registered XA-SIA, on 3 April; TriStars of Court Line on training flights in May; Indian Air Force Constellation BG583 on 31 July for attention by Aviation Traders; and French Air Force Caravelle 116 on 21 November. In 1974 significant visitors included two Tu.134 aircraft of the East German airline Interflug which appeared on 24 April from Leipzig with football fans. Another unusual visitor was a Dakota 3 of the Finnish Air Force, serialled Do.10, on 6 May, while two Il.62s of Aeroflot, CCCP-86681 and 86697, appeared on 26 June after diverting from Heathrow.

Court Line's pink Tristar G-BAAB 'Halcyon Breeze' on finals during an evening training sortie at Stansted. [via P. Kemp]

INTO THE SEVENTIES

The Luton-based Court Line Aviation used Stansted for training and some charters. Left, at the hold for 05 is Court Line's BAC-111/518FG G-AXMF named 'Halcyon Breeze'.

New to Stansted in 1974 was Tempair International Airlines, a subsidiary of Templewood Aviation Ltd., which had been founded in 1967 to provide aircraft and crews on a contract basis. On 21 October a Boeing 707-321, 9G-ACB, arrived, followed in November by 9G-ACD. The Company opened a small office at Stansted and its aircraft were looked after by Aviation Traders.

Army helicopters were seen at Stansted on 3 February 1974 in a search for thieves who, posing as members of the IRA, had made off with £35,000 from the National Westminster Bank in the terminal. A year later at Chelmsford Crown Court two airport employees, one a fireman and the other a duty officer, were sentenced to ten years imprisonment for the crime.

Trans Meridian Air Cargo maintained its activities through the early 'seventies, and in May 1974 opened a regular freight service to Amsterdam, Bahrain and Hong Kong. A year later a CL-44 weekly freight run to Kano and Lagos from Stansted, Ostend, Rotterdam and Basle as required was inaugurated. This was named the 'Impala' service, while the 'Ghengis Khan' service was flown from the same departure points to Istanbul, Nicosia, Kuwait, Bahrain, Abu Dhabi, Karachi, Delhi and points east.

Maplin project scrapped

On the very day on which the BAA's 1974 report was published, 18 July, the Government announced that Maplin was to be abandoned as the site for a third London airport. A committee set up to determine if Maplin was still necessary had advised Peter Shore MP, the Secretary of State for Trade, that a number of trends which showed that exisiting airports could handle the projected air traffic until 1990 at the earliest had been discovered; significant reductions in forecast passenger growth and in take-offs and landings (due to the 1973 oil crisis) and a large reduction in the noise problem. An airport at Maplin Sands was no longer seen as viable, due to its capital cost and the time which would be taken to build it. Nigel Foulkes, Chairman of BAA, described Stansted as being the 'expansion chamber' of the south-east. A newspaper leader, however, commented that Stansted's under-used facilities were valuable not as the basis of a major new airport but as spare capacity pending clarification of future requirements. Responding to the BAA report and the official decision, Geoffrey Waterer, Chairman of Essex County Council, said that his Council would seek clear limitations from the Government on the growth of Stansted, with parameters to be known to all concerned in advance. *"So far as the Essex County Council is concerned,"* he said, *"if Stansted is going to be an 'expansion chamber' at all it is going to be a very small one and it is going to be built to very exacting standards so that it does not burst. The specification must not include elastic sides."* A week later, the Council stated that it was prepared for limited expansion to allow Stansted to become the third London airport, but was determined to resist growth anything like that at Gatwick.

The very striking DC-8-33 G-BETS, one of the few examples of Douglas' four engined airliners to be operated by a U.K. airline. Formerly used by African Safari and for a short time Transmed, it was withdrawn from service for use as spares until ending its days as a fire training aircraft.[via P. Kemp]

THE STANSTED EXPERIENCE

DC-9-15 I-TIGE of Aerolinee Itavia touches down at Stansted on 3 November 1974. [T. Harding]

Laker's 'Skytrain' service across the Atlantic, which would have been a blessing to Stansted, still failed to materialise in 1974 as US approval had not been received. Most airline movements in and out of Stansted continued to be by foreign airlines, particularly from the Scandinavian countries. The few IT charters flown during 1974 included Trans Europa Caravelles flying three trips per week on behalf of Tom Hill Holidays. Overall, air transport flights remained static in number at about four per day on average. Visitors of a more interesting nature in 1974 included a number of Tu.134s, Il.18s and Il.62s from East Germany which brought football supporters on two occasions in March and April, and Grumman Goose amphibian N2721A on its delivery flight from the USA to Tasman Airlines in Australia. This unusual visitor was at Stansted between 16 and 28 August, when it left for Lyons on the next leg of its trip. Overseas National and Pacific Western were other airlines which sent aircraft — DC-8s, DC-10s and Boeing 707s — to Stansted regularly during 1974.

Hijack!

Without doubt the main event of 1975 was the hijacking between Manchester and Heathrow of British Airways' flight BE4069 on 7 January.

Although he wanted to bow to the demand of the hijacker (Saaed Madjd) that he be flown to France, Capt. Harry Lea was ordered to land it at Stansted, and did so at 23.25 hours. By that time, Stansted and its approach roads had been closed to the general public and an attempt had been made to disguise the terminal as Orly airport, Paris! Before the arrival of the BAC One-Eleven (G-AVMP), a Trident carrying BA directors and a number of policemen had arrived, as had an army Scout helicopter and an RAF Hercules believed to have brought SAS and other troops to the scene. After landing, the One-Eleven taxied to the Fordair hangar, where the hijacker disembarked with his hostage, a steward. Police than moved in and, after a scuffle, arrested the culprit, a police dog biting the steward in the process. After this unwanted event, the Chief Constable of Essex, Sir John Nightingale, said that the response at Stansted had been a great success, and he was indebted to Insp. Arthur Mason, head of the airport police, who set up the control for the operation.

By February 1975, Stansted was yet again being considered for significant expansion. This time a committee set up by the Government, consisting of representatives from the Department of Trade, the Department of the Environment,

Parked on the apron in front to Stansted's old terminal, Balkan Airlines' Tu.154B LZ-BTS is seen awaiting passengers on the inaugural flight of the service. [Stansted Airport Ltd.]

INTO THE SEVENTIES

Left: Boeing 737-2K2C
PH-TVC of Transavia
Holland.

Below: Falconair Electra
SE-FGB Sky Express.

BAA, CAA and other organisations, was briefed to evaluate Stansted. Following the collapse of Channel Airways and Lloyd International, the airport was handling only about 200,000 passengers per year, but was considered to have a capacity of 3 million without any alteration. Almost at once, Robert McCrindle MP (Con., Brentwood & Ongar) tabled a Commons question, asking for assurance that Stansted was not being considered again for substantial development. It was to be nearly two years before that question could be answered properly.

There was still no news of the projected Laker 'Skytrain' service, but on 7 February 1975 the CAA did begin to support the idea officially, condemning the negative response given to the application by the American authorities. Fares would be raised to £52 one-way for summer flights and £59 during the winter. On 29 July, however, after a change of Government and with general economic conditions acting against the project, the Secretary of State for Trade announced that, after all, British Airways was to retain its monopoly status over the Atlantic!

Harking back to an earlier era is this pair of C-47s.

Dakota (C-47A) G-AGJV of Air Anglia at Stansted in the early seventies.

Dakota G-AMPO of Macedonian Aviation.

THE STANSTED EXPERIENCE

Fairly frequent visitors to Stansted were the Viscounts of the Turkish Air Force, THK, following their re-sparring by Aviation Traders. This example is serialled 430. [P. Kemp]

Although no passenger airlines were based at Stansted, inbound charter business increased a little in 1975, Sunday mornings being the busiest period of the week. Flights from Scandinavia in particular helped to expand the number of passengers handled, but several American airlines, including Capitol, Flying Tigers and Airlift, also contributed to the upturn. Transmeridian Air Cargo remained busy, its CL-44s operating to North Africa and the Far East in particular.

Aviation Traders continued to expand, and in July moved its components manufacturing operation from Southend into Hangar 1. Although most of ATEL's work still involved Boeing 707s, a number of ex-RAF Britannias came throught the workshops toward the end of 1975 before being sold to civilian freight airlines such as Young Cargo of Belgium. Further Britannias arrived early in 1976 from storage at RAF Kemble. Also passing through ATEL's hands were three ex-Turk Hava Yollari Viscounts (246, 430 and 431) which had to be re-sparred before transfer to the Turkish Air Force.

Early in 1976, Fordair began looking at alternative, larger, aircraft to cope with the growing demand for its private scheduled services. The choice was the BAC One-Eleven, and two such aircraft were purchased from the Brazilian Air Force. The first one, VC92-2110/G-BEJM, arrived at Stansted on 5 December 1976, and the task of converting eighteen flight-deck crews to the type began. The second aircraft, VC92-2111/G-BEJW, was sent to the United States for refurbishment into the standard 40-seat layout and returned to Stansted on 31 July 1977. Later that year, a third BAC 1-11, G-BFMC, was bought from German airline Bavaria, and after refurbishment entered service in March 1978. The first 1-11 was then reconfigured as an 18-seat executive aircraft. During 1979, over 58,000 passengers were carried by the six-aircraft fleet, and twenty pilots and nine cabin staff were now employed by Fordair.

Members of Essex County Council were notified in the early days of 1976 that BAA appeared to be thinking in terms of expansion of passenger throughput to 16 million, which was equivalent to the 1971 Heathrow figure. Councillor Derek Wood, who had been prominent in the anti-Maplin campaign, proposed that the Council should approve development

Left: From what was then the wrong side of the Iron Curtain, LOT Polish Airlines sent IL-18 SP-LSF to Stansted in May 1979. [via P. Kemp]

Right: Once quite common at Stansted was the Caravelle, here exemplified by Finnair's OH-LSG. The date was September 1979. [via P. Kemp]

British Airways aircraft started appearing more and more at Stansted during the 1970's with 737-2K2C PH-TVE (right) on lease to fly some of their charter work, whilst (below) 747-236 G-BDXB was on crew-training. In the background can be seen Fordair's G-BEJW. [via P. Kemp]

allowing passenger numbers to rise to but not to exceed 4 million. During 1975 Stansted handled 238,000 passengers, an increase of 19.5% over the previous year, plus 19,600 tonnes of cargo, 18% more than in 1974.

Regular flights into Stansted during 1976 remained at the same level as in the previous year, but there were a number of proposals by other airlines which said that they wanted to use Stansted. Among them was El Al, the Israeli airline, which put forward a plan to fly fruit in daily, but as adequate security could not be guaranteed the idea was dropped. A regular visitor was Boeing 707 5X-UAL of Uganda Airlines, which flew freight from Stansted for the benefit of President Idi Amin. This aircraft touched down at Stansted on 15 July carrying three crates which were not listed on the manifest. The media speculated that they contained radars damaged during the Israeli attack on Entebbe, for repair in the UK, and although nothing was proved, there were calls for a ban on such flights. Overall, following a decided drop in the number of training flights during the year, the number of movements in 1976 fell by about 17% compared with 1975 and 33% compared with five years previously. These were not happy days at Stansted. On the brighter side, Aviation Traders & Engineering Ltd., by now owned by Aer Lingus, transferred the last of its operation from Southend on 18 June 1976.

Instone Airline, acting as aircraft brokers, was not finding much racehorse traffic during the early winter of 1976/7 so carried car parts from Bristol to Cologne for Fords and became involved in oil-related charter work. Air Atlantique was carrying mail from Stansted to Liverpool in their Dakotas, and on 14 December 1976 Jersey European Airlines opened a Stansted to Liverpool service using Bandeirante aircraft. JEA's Stansted to Jersey service now flew via Shoreham. Scheduled departures from Stansted at the end of the year comprised six on Mondays, two on Tuesdays and Thursdays, four on Wednesdays, five on Fridays, three on Saturdays and no less than ten on Sundays. Not exactly the busiest airport in Britain!

The Skytrain saga was not yet over, as on 15 December 1976 it was ruled by the Court of Appeal that Secretary of State Peter Shore had gone beyond his legal powers in favouring the BA monopoly at the expense of Skytrain. Freddie Laker then stated that he could inaugurate his service within a month of being given final approval, but doubts whether Skytrain would ever get off the ground persisted.

Improvements made

Neverthless, work on a 600 sq.m. (6456 sq.ft.) extension to the terminal building went ahead at the end of 1976, providing better baggage reclaim facilities and a covered walkway from the building to the aircraft stands. At the same time, plans for a completely new terminal were prepared but were not put out to tender until such development could be justified. Passenger figures had fallen since 1975, but BAA was still aiming to increase the number by a factor of 24 to 6

A view of the apron one fine day in October 1977 reveals BA Tristar G-BEAK, a BA Trident, a Boeing 737 of Maersk, an Aviaco DC9 and two 737s of Britannia Airways, a KLM DC-8 and an ex-RAF Britannia. The TriStar, Trident and DC8 were diversions from Heathrow, the Britannia and 737s diversions from Luton. [via P. Kemp]

million by 1990. Fewer complaints about noise, 53 altogether, were received in 1975, 22 of them from the same Hatfield Broad Oak resident! January 1977 passengers totalled 19,500, most of them Scandinavian, an increase of 93.6% over the previous January. The immediate aim was to increase passengers to one million per year, services to be attracted from Heathrow and Gatwick by low landing fees, but Donald Turner, the BAA's Director of Planning, said on London Weekend TV on 17 April that with its present single runway and land area Stansted could cope with 15 to 16 million passengers per year by the mid-1980s. He mentioned that a White Paper expected soon would authorise the first stage of development at Stansted.

On 14 February Edmund Dell MP, the new Secretary of State for Trade, told MPs that he had decided not to appeal against the Court of Appeal's decision in favour of the Skytrain service, thus ending the years of legal conflict and indecision on the subject. At long last it was announced on 14 June that the 'Skytrain' service would begin to operate on 26 September 1977

between Stansted and New York, but after pressure brought by Freddie Laker, the CAA acceded to his request for Skytrain restrictions to be removed and allowed the service to use Gatwick instead of Stansted. This was of course a major blow for Stansted, as high hopes had been placed on this and similar schemes coming to fruition.

Summer 1977 activity was almost all at weekends, with inbound charter flights from Scandinavia prominent. On Friday evenings, three Boeing 737s of Braathens SAFE, a Boeing 720 of Conair and a DC-8 of Scanair could be seen, while Saturday brought Fokker F-28s of Braathens and Linjerflyg, DC-9s of Scanair and a Boeing 707 of Air Malta to Stansted. There was even more to see on Sundays, when four F-28s of Linjeflyg, two Boeing 707s of Conair, two Boeing 737s of Braathens, two DC-8s or DC-9s of Scanair, a Boeing 727 of Transair, a Boeing 737 of Maersk and a DC-8 or Caravelle of Aviaco usually appeared. Then Stansted settled down to await the influx of passengers on the following Friday, briefly dealing with British

An un-missable shape on the apron at Stansted was Boeing 747-227 N601BN 'Big Orange' of Braniff International Airlines' seen here in October 1978. [via P. Kemp]

INTO THE SEVENTIES

...and of course Air Atlantique operated DC-6B with the appropriate registration G-SIXB at Stansted for a while.
[both via P. Kemp]

Midland flights to Jersey and East Midlands and an Austrian Airlines DC-9 in the meantime!

Transmeridian Air Cargo, part of the T.D.Keegan Group, was sold to Cunard Shipping Co. Ltd., part of the Trafalgar House Group, in June 1977 for £3,370,000. The airline suffered a setback on 2 September, when its CL-44-D4 freighter G-ATZH crashed into the sea after take-off from Kai Tak Airport, Hong Kong, with the loss of all four of the crew. In 1978 a associated Company, TAC Heavylift, was formed. Transmeridian itself merged on 20 August 1979 with IAS Cargo to form British Cargo Airlines. Trafalgar House owned a two-thirds interest in TAC Heavylift, while the remainder was held by Eurolatin Aviation, which promptly bought three redundant Belfast freight aircraft from the RAF and contracted with Marshall of Cambridge to modify them and to secure a civilian operating certificate.

The first visit by a Boeing 747 of South African Airways was made on 10 January 1977, when 747-244B ZS-SAO arrived at Stansted when diverted from Heathrow due to a baggage

Reminiscent of an earlier age was Convair 340 SE-GTE of Scanbee, modified with a 'thimble' radar nose, which visited Stansted in October 1978. [via P. Kemp]

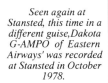

Seen again at Stansted, this time in a different guise,Dakota G-AMPO of Eastern Airways' was recorded at Stansted in October 1978.

Conroy Aircraft Corporation's unique CL44 'Skymonster' conversion N447T operated by Transmeridian Air Cargo demonstrates it's load-carrying capability for the camera.

A colourful aircraft seen against a threatening sky at Stansted in June 1978: Uganda Airlines Boeing 707 N794RN. [via P. Kemp]

handlers' dispute. Two weeks later, Israeli C-130H Hercules 4X-FBU found itself parked next to Idi Amin's L-100-30 Hercules 5X-UCF, an embarassing situation for the airport authority! The first A.300 Airbus to visit Stansted appeared on 3 March 1977, when OO-TEG of TEA landed. Although Boeing 707s remained the main interest at Aviation Traders in 1977, 727s, DC-8s and VC-10s were also dealt with, the latter comrising four ex-Gulf Air aircraft for storage and eventual resale.

The vexed question of development at Stansted was debated at a conference organised by the Regional Studies Association on 12 January 1978. Peter Hall of Reading University told the meeting that Stansted was wanted as the third London airport by the Department of Transport, the airlines, BAA and CAA, and could be developed incrementally to meet evolving demands. The airport, he said, had a railway spur that if reopened could allow trains to run to Liverpool Street station in forty minutes. It appears that Mr Hall was thinking of the Bishops Stortford to Braintree branch line which was still open at that time for freight and ran parallel to the A120, passing very close to the airfield. Work, said Mr. Hall, could be provided for people living in the run-down East End communities. However, he considered that development would spoil one of the few really open and quiet rural communities within forty miles of central London. *"It is difficult to avoid the conclusion"*, he said enigmatically, *"that the air interests are proceeding by stealth, fortified by the bleak climate of public expenditure cuts..."*.

Aircraft movements remained much the same in 1977 as in the previous year, but in 1978 a marked increase in private and flying club use of the airport accounted for an increase of 10% in the total. Although Sterling and Maersk both decided to make greater use of Luton during the year, Maersk continued to fly some charters into

Stansted has long been used as a temporary base for the RAF's Red Arrows demonstration team when giving displays at local airfields. In July 1978 the team was still using Gnat aircraft, which are seen here parked awaiting the day's work. [via P. Kemp]

Scenes no more!

Left: Britannia G-AOVS of Redcoat, May 1978. [via P. Kemp]

Below: Laker Airways Boeing 707-138B G-AVZZ seen at Stansted in June 1978 [via P. Kemp]

Left: Far from home, Lockheed L-1049C BG581 of the Indian Air Force heads for touchdown at a sunny Stansted. [via P. Kemp]

This picture: Carrying the 'last two' as initials of its travel boss Harry Goodman, Boeing 737-253 G-BMHG of the now-defunct Air Europe, seen at Stansted in May 1979. [via P. Kemp]

THE STANSTED EXPERIENCE

Right: The Argentinian Air Force (FAA) regularly sent C-130 aircraft to Stansted to collect equipment and armaments. Here C-130 TC-68 is seen awaiting attention in the rain in September 1978.

Below: Often seen at Stansted in pre-Falklands War days were the 707s of the Argentinian Air Force. Here TC-82 is being loaded with a cargo of military supplies. [via P. Kemp]

Stansted. Other airlines operating from Scandinavia included Linjeflyg, six of whose Fokker F-28s flew twelve trips into Stansted on one busy day. Optimism was in the air, as Air Anglia announced its plans to use Stansted for up to 21 flights per week to Brussels, beginning in the spring of 1979, and for a service to Aberdeen, which began on 1 November 1978. Other proposals, which failed to mature, were from British Air Ferries, which wanted to operate to Brussels, Dublin, Jersey, Guernsey, Frankfurt, Paris and Zurich using Boeing 727s, and from Dan-Air, which proposed a service to Amsterdam. Permission was given to Intra Airways to operate to Jersey. Freight carrier Bamberg International Sky Karriers [sic] wished to fly freight from Stansted but this scheme never materialised.

The first of three trial flights from Stansted by Britannia Airways took place on 26 February 1978, when Boeing 737-204 G-BAZG took off for Palma, Majorca. However, as the service had not been adequately publicised, two further flights were cancelled. On the day after the trial flight, BAC 1-11-518 G-AXMG of Britannia's competitor, Monarch Airlines, suffered a collapsed undercarriage on Stansted's runway, which was blocked for sixteen hours. Only the crew of three was on board at the time.

Although in 1976 El Al had decided not to use Stansted, the airline began weekly charter flights from Tel Aviv on 26 April 1978, using Boeing 707s. Security at the airport was intense, and the authorities were commended by the airline, which was very impressed by the service it received. Nigeria Airways was another airline to use the airport in 1978 for a series of charters, and the Tu.134s of Aviogenex were also seen

Boeing 737 G-AXNC of Britannia Airways.

Whoops! Monarch Airlines' BAC 1-11-518 G-AXMG after coming to grief on Stansted's runway in February 1978. There was little damage, and the aircraft soon flew again. [via P. Kemp]

once a week.

As part of a publicity campaign under the headline 'Fly Stansted', planned to entice more IT flights to the airport, Boeing B-17G G-BEDF was present on 4 August. Among other aircraft visiting Stansted in 1978 were a Polish-registered Mi.2 helicopter, 544538125/SP-SWG, which was being used by Ursus-Bizon (UK) Ltd. at Needham Market; two CASA 212 Aviocars (145 and 146) which called in on their way from Spain on delivery to the Chilean Navy on 5 August; and two aircraft, Boeing 707 N64740 and DC-8-21 N8033U, which flew Vietnamese refugees in on 16 October. From late August, however, the Home Office applied tighter security measures and the public could no longer have an adequate view of these choice machines.

Probably the busiest day in Stansted's civilian history so far, in terms of passengers handled, was 23 August 1978, when a strike of engineers at Heathrow took place. Stansted accepted thirteen diversions, eight of them Boeing 747s, of which four were on Stansted's apron at the same time. Extra passengers dealt with totalled 4876.

A major landmark was the addition of Stansted as the southern terminus of Air Anglia's route from Norwich to Leeds/Bradford, Edinburgh and Aberdeen, which took place on 1 November 1978 with the departure of Friendship 200 G-BDDH. The Friendships used continued to dominate the scheduled services at Stansted in 1979, with three flights each day to Aberdeen.

After a Boeing 707 of Uganda Airlines skidded off Stansted's runway into snow on 24

Transmeridian's CL-44 G-AZIN at Stansted in January 1979. [via P. Kemp]

On a snowy January day in 1979, ex-RAF Belfast XR362 awaits civilianisation for Transmeridian Air Cargo. Named 'Samson' by the RAF, this aircraft became G-BEPE. [via P. Kemp]

British Island Airways' Bandeirante G-OAIR at Stansted in September 1979 [via P. Kemp]

Air Anglia's first twin-jet Fokker F-28 Mk.1000 Fellowship was PH-MOL leased from the manufacturers before delivery of their own Mk.4000s. This type and its derivatives, in service with Air Anglia's successors would play a major part in Stansted's scheduled service expansion. [VFW Fokker]

January 1979, questions were asked in high places about the twice-weekly trips flown by the airline to Kampala. It was alleged that these flights, known locally as 'the whiskey run', carried luxury goods for the benefit of President Idi Amin as well as the bona-fide cargo of British goods. On 27 February Uganda Airlines denied that any spirits had been carried since three large consignments were photographed being loaded eighteen months earlier. However, on 5 March, the Government banned all Uganda Airlines cargo flights.

In August 1979, work began on resurfacing Stansted's runway, which involved closing the airport between 22.00 and 07.00 each night during the week and prohibiting use of the airfield for crew training in any aircraft larger that a Herald. This task was not completed by the end of the year and the remaining work was therefore postponed for a few months. The quota of night flights by aircraft classed as 'noisy' was increased by 50%, allowing 180 slots in the winter of 1978/79 and 450 slots for the period April to October 1979. All noisy aircraft were to be phased out by 1987, however.

As the year, and the decade, came to an end, Stansted was once more being promoted as the site for the third airport for the London area. The first talk of a new terminal to handle 15 million passengers per year and of a rail link into the airport was heard, but the fact remained that Stansted was still operating far below its capacity.

Chapter Seven

Hopes for the Future

During the autumn of 1979, a merger between Air Anglia, British Island Airways, Air Wales and Air West had been announced, the resultant company (a subsidiary of British Air Transport Holdings Ltd.) to be known as Air UK, a name which has since become extremely well-known at Stansted and many other airports. So it was that Air UK, with headquarters at Norwich, came into being on 1 January 1980 with a fleet of twenty Heralds, ten Fokker F-27 Friendships, six Bandeirantes, four BAC 1-11s and two Fokker F-28 Fellowships. One of the new airline's routes was from Stansted to Aberdeen via Norwich and Leeds, though this was soon closed, a significant number of employees losing their jobs. British Island Airways had been interested in using Stansted before the merger, but its application for services to Paris and Jersey had been rejected by the CAA, the latter because it was felt that the current licence-holder, British Midland, could easily cope with any increase in traffic to the

island. Nevertheless, during the year Jersey European was given a licence to fly to Jersey, using Herald aircraft, from Stansted — the only scheduled service from the airport at the time!

TAC Heavylift unveiled on 6 March the first of the three Belfast freight aircraft which had been purchased from the RAF, G-BEPE, and announced that the aircraft could carry up to 34 tons of cargo in its 11,000 cubic foot (311.5 cub. m.) hold. The Certificate of Airworthiness was handed over by Mr. J. Simpson of the CAA to Capt. P. J. McGoldrick, Managing Director of TAC Heavylift. In three years, £4 million had been spent to achieve certification. As part of a new image, TAC Heavylift changed its name on 1 September 1980 to Heavylift Cargo Airlines. Among the loads flown by the airline during this period were three Sea King helicopters, IN551-553, carried out to India for use by the Indian Navy.

Industrial action by maintenance personnel at

Stansted from the air, seen just as the first vestiges of the M11 Motorway were beginning to appear on the landscape - seen at the top of this picture.

THE STANSTED EXPERIENCE

A pilots-eye view of the approach to runway 05 in about 1980. The hangar used by Fordair is off to the right, with the passenger terminal complex to the left. [Reg Pannell]

Heathrow brought diversions to Stansted on 10 January, prominent among which were two Concordes, the first of the type to visit. Other types included VC-10s and Boeing 747s, but none could match the thrill of seeing the supersonic Concorde for the first time.

Coincident with the success of Heavylift was the demise in March 1980 of its associated Company, British Cargo Airlines, whose three DC-8s, normally flown from Gatwick, went into store at Stansted. One of BCA's most important contracts had been the delivery of components for BAC 1-11 aircraft to Rumania for final assembly. Two more Belfasts were purchased by Heavylift in July 1980, this time from Rolls-Royce, which had bought them from the RAF for the sake of the engines but later decided not to retain them. At much the same time, the second Belfast, G-BEPS, entered service.

Sunday was probably the busiest day of the week at this time, with twelve flights by Braathens 737s, Scanair DC-8s and DC-9s, Conair Boeing 720s and one of Jersey European's Heralds. It was expected that Maersk Air would return to Stansted to operate six flights each day during the summer for students visiting this country. Aviogenex was flying twice a week to Belgrade, while Air Zaire planned to fly car components several times per week to Kinshasa on behalf of British Leyland.

The development question still unresolved

Interested parties attending a seminar organised by the Royal Town Planning Institute on 5 February 1980 were told that the choice of Stansted as London's third airport ignored hidden urbanisation costs. Derek Senior of the RTPI said that no less than 70,000 extra houses would be needed at Stansted compared with only 40,000 near an airport at Maplin. Furthermore, agricultural land absorbed for the development of Stansted would total 6000 hectares (14820 acres) against 2000 hectares (4940 acres) at Maplin. Reacting to these figures, the Chaiman of BAA, Norman Payne, stated on 11 March that Stansted was chosen to take overflow traffic from Heathrow and Gatwick and could be staffed adequately without creating any new towns or covering Essex with concrete. BAA, he said, was aware of the need to restrict airport activities to

Concorde G-BOAF exciting considerable interest when it visited Stansted. Sterling Airways Boeing 727 'Skybus' looks on.

Take the Blue Plane! With the emergence of Air UK from the amalgamation of a number of airlines, a new colour scheme was to be seen at Stansted. Left: 1-11 G-CBIA 'Island Ensign', below; Fokker F-27 B-BAUR.

within the airport boundary, unlike the situation at Heathrow, where a number of hotels had been built along the Bath Road, which forms the northern edge of that airport.

Having been invited by the Government to bring forward any proposals for expansion at Stansted to handle 15 million passengers per year (provided the existing runway could be used), BAA published details of the first stage on 22 April 1980 and submitted a planning application to Uttlesford District Council on 25 July. The development proposed covered 957.5 hectares (2365 acres), of which 366 hectares (904 acres) were already owned by BAA. Within the area earmarked for the new terminal building were 23 houses and 285 'mobile homes'. Cost of the development would be £350 million, and initially 20,000 jobs would be created, of which a quarter

would be for people in the 16-24 age group. Construction could start in 1983. As there was a great deal of opposition to the proposal from the relevant Local Authorities and residents, a public enquiry was expected to be held in 1981. The Chairman of BAA said *"We are very anxious to tell people about our plans as soon as possible. It is right that they should have the facts as soon as they are available so that they know where they stand."* It was ironic that just at this time passenger throughput at Stansted fell by nearly 25%, largely due to the poor state of the economy in Scandinavian countries, and cargo handled dropped by 60%.

Another objector to the proposed development was the Countryside Commission, which on 27 June 1980 expressed fears that environmental destruction would result. Lord Winstanley, the

Laker Skytrain DC-10 G-BELO landing at Stansted [via P. Kemp]

Facilities in the old terminal building left something to be desired when compared with the new terminal. Here, passengers await check-in for Air UK, Jersey European and Dan-Air flights. [Stansted Airport Ltd.]

Commission's Chairman, in a letter to the Secretary of State for the Environment (Michael Heseltine MP), wrote that the proposed airport *"would constitute a massive urbanisation of an attractive area of countryside."* The Country Landowners Association was also against any development, and on 24 September 1980 accused the Government of concealing the full social and environmental impilcations of the proposed development. According to the CLA's President, George Lillingston, about 4000 acres (1620 hectares) of high-grade land would be swallowed up by first-stage extensions to the airport, apart from land for industry and housing. At least two new towns would be built, covering an area three times that of Harlow New Town! Members of the CLA pledged themselves to oppose by every possible means *"...the physical and psychological rape of a tranquil and beautiful*

part of Essex." Robin Neville, a member of the CLA's Essex committee, said that the local inhabitants, who had twice before successfully opposed the designation of Stansted as London's third airport, were ready to defend their interests again. While these statements were being made, Aviation Traders applied for permission to erect a new hangar to cater for Boeing 747 servicing contracts which were being negotiated, two 747s at a time being expected.

Meanwhile, the routine at Stansted continued. Southern International began flying a Viscount to Belfast from Stansted every night with newspapers, although the airline's maintenance base remained at Southampton. Two DC-9s were on order for planned IT work, as well as more Viscounts. Other regular flights from Stansted in 1980 included Air Malta Boeing 737s between May and October, Tarom Tu.154s from May to

CL-44D-4 N122AE of Air Express International, named "Dixie", taxying from the end of runway 23 to the cargo area. [via P. Kemp]

These temporary buildngs were among many originally used by the TAD which saw post-war service and survived into the nineteen-eighties. (Right to left): building 30, (a Robin hangar) a salvage store; building 28, an ordnance armoury store; building 29 (another Robin hangar) the propellor shop. The building on the left seems to be a later addition. Behind is the double E.D.D. type building used by the TAD as an assembly shop. [P. Francis]

September, and over the winter season Balkan Tu.154s to Plovdiv between December 1980 and the following April. An Air France Concorde put in an appearance on 16 November from Paris/Charles de Gaulle, carrying 99 passengers who were exchanged for 99 others for the return journey. Several Saab 105 training aircraft of the Swedish Air Force were also seen that month, their pilots making use of the chance to fly commercial air routes to help them convert to civil aviation procedures before they left the service. The Christmas period saw five football charters from Nigeria at Stansted.

Public enquiry planned
BAA's planning application was called in by Michael Heseltine MP on 3 December 1980, and a public enquiry to commence at Charrington House in Bishops Stortford in September 1981 under the Chairmanship of Graham Eyre QC was announced. In a statement on 3 February 1981, BAA denied that development of Stansted to handle 15 million passengers per year would

involve the construction of a new town. To meet the criteria, a new terminal building would be needed, with stands for up to fifty aircraft, and short-term parking for 4000 cars. A 350-bedroom hotel would be built, and up to 6000 new houses would be needed. Two farms would close as they were within the 1500 acres (607 hectares) earmarked for development. At this, the Chairman of the Preservation Association, John Lukies, commented *"We still feel it is iniquitous that we should have to fight the battle again — Stansted has twice been rejected... at a public enquiry — but fight we will."*

About 200 members of bodies which were objecting to the Stansted development held a silent protest outside Saffron Walden town hall on 3 April 1981. Inside, a preliminary meeting was being held inside for organisations which wished to present themselves at the forthcoming public enquiry, which was likely to last up to a year and cost £4 million. By this time, the Preservation Association had raised over £100,000 with which to fight its case, and

Three ordnance armoury store buildings type U.S.T., buildings 23 to 25, in use for other purposes in the 1980s. [P. Francis]

THE STANSTED EXPERIENCE

Left: Nigerian Navy Lynx 02-F89 being loaded onto Heavylift Belfast.

crop-sprayers and a C-130 fuselage from Sao Tome to Venice. More mundanely, mining gear was flown from Dusseldorf to Lusaka, tin cans to Lagos and cement from Milan to Algeria. By June 1981, Heavylift was carrying Boeing 767 components from Naples to Seattle for assembly, BAC 1-11 fuselages from Bournemouth (Hurn) to Bucharest and Jaguar components from Warton to Bangalore for assembly by Hindustan Aircraft.

Aviation Traders & Engineering Ltd., which employed 500 people, won the Queen's Award for Export Achievement in 1981 but its application for permission to build a new hangar in which to expand its Boeing maintenance work was rejected by Uttlesford District Council as it was considered to be part of an unapproved airport development programme. Nevertheless, an extension to the terminal building was already being carried out, and Plessey AR.1 radar (which had been transferred from Wraith Hill in Scotland) became operational in the new radar room in April 1981. This equipment gave a range of 50 miles (80km.) with a height ceiling of 12,000 feet (3650m.).

opposition was being coordinated. Somewhat surprisingly, among those opposed to the scheme was British Airways, which was pressing for further development at Heathrow and was expected to influence the opinions of other airlines.

Early in 1981 a Heavylift Belfast flew to Singapore to carry out a number of mercy missions to Phnom Penh in Kampuchea on behalf of Oxfam and other organisations, the main loads being trucks for use in distribution of supplies. Flights were also made from Singapore to Australia, the first on 27 February. Three Puma helicopters were transported from Marseilles to Indonesia in the capacious holds of Belfast aircraft, as were three Bell 47s to Cairo for use as

Return of a historic airline

An old friend re-appeared at Stansted on 13 March 1981 in the form of a Bristol Freighter, or 'Bristol Vibrator' as it was affectionately known by pilots. Although destined for Instone Air Line, this aircraft was still registered in New Zealand as ZK-EPH after service with the RNZAF as NZ5912. The intention was to use this and possibly three similar aircraft on racehorse traffic within the UK and to and from Continental

Tri-engined differences!

Left: Dan-Air's Boeing 727-95 G-BFGN climbs out into the evening sun...

... whilst a long way from home in the Channel Islands, Aurigny Trislander G-AYWI rests between flights

HOPES FOR THE FUTURE

Instone Air Line's Bristol Freighter G-BISU.

Zimbabwe-based cargo airline Afretair brought their DC-8-55F TR-LVK to the freight apron at Stansted.

destinations. To promote this service, Instone opened an office at Stansted in June, and ZK-EPH soon became G-BISU. Instone carried out its first task with the Freighter on 3 August 1981, when it flew racehorses from Deauville to Stansted, where they were collected by road transport for onward carriage to Newmarket. A second Freighter, G-AMLK (ex ZK-EPD) arrived on 23 August 1982.

A welcome new arrival at Stansted in March 1981 was Sterling Airways, which announced its transfer from Luton. Sterling's service was inaugurated on 3 April, the first of five flights planned each week, using Caravelles or Boeing 727s. Another piece of good news was the award to Air UK of a licence to operate a service to Paris (Orly), signifying the recommencement of that airline's activities at Stansted. For the summer of 1981, Tarom flew a weekly service to Constanta in Bulgaria with Tu.154s, while Transeuropa, which moved its operation from Southend, used Caravelles on a service to Palma each week. Every other week saw Air Malta Boeing 720s depart for Luqa, and on Friday and Sunday evenings Conair maintained its Scandinavian service with Boeing 720s, although the Sunday service came to an end in July 1981 after seven years due to lack of demand. Scanair also ended its Sunday evening service for the same reason. From July to the end of October Britannia Airways Boeing 737s were evident at Stansted on an IT service to Palma.

One of the regular sights (and sounds!) at Stansted for a number of years had been Piaggio 166 G-APWY, used by Marconi Avionics to calibrate their trial radar installation at nearby

Britannia's 737-204 G-BGYK 'R.J. Mitchell' sweeps into land at the end of another IT charter.

THE STANSTED EXPERIENCE

Laker Airways' Airbus A.300 G-BIMC "Intercity Express" at Stansted on 17 June 1983.

Matching, but on 19 February 1981 this aircraft was retired and was presented to the Southend Historic Aircraft Museum.

In March, the last Doves operated by the CAA Flying Unit also departed, after many years' service, leaving the two Avro 748s as the main workhorses, their primary function being to calibrate and test radar and radio navigational aids provided by National Air Traffic Services at airports around Great Britain. In addition, flight testing of candidates for the initial issue of professional pilots' licences, instrument ratings and instructors' ratings was carried out, with a number of subsidiary tasks completing the work. Apart from the equipment needed for safe operation of the aircraft, each was provided with a wide variety of calibrated equipment such as DME (Distance Measuring Equipment), 360-channel VHF radio, UHF radio, ADF (Automatic Direction Finder), ILS (Instrument Landing System) and VOR (Voice Omni-directional Radio Range).

A typical task was the routine inspection of an ILS system at, say, Luton airport. Planning began on the previous day, when the Senior Navigation Aid Inspector and his assistants decided the priority of work and the operations section allocated the two flight-deck crew. After engineers finished their routine pre-flight inspection and specialists from the CAFU Standards Laboratory completed their calibration, the aircraft would take off, and for the next three or four hours carried out the laid-down procedures, flying down the beam to about fifty feet (15m.) above the ground, the entire manoeuvre being co-ordinated by Luton air traffic control. Over the next few days, the data gathered and recorded was analysed and compared with film taken by the fuselage-mounted camera.

Several flights were diverted to Stansted due to an air traffic controllers' strike at Heathrow and West Drayton on 21 May 1981. Aircraft types seen at Stansted that day included Air France Boeing 727s and Fokker 28s, KLM DC-10, LOT Tu.134, British Airways TriStar, and Iberia DC-9 and DC-10. Examples of the Argentinian Air Force fleet could still be seen at Stansted in those pre-Falkland days collecting munitions, and their Boeing 707s TC-91 and TC-93 were in evidence.

On 27 May the new extension to the terminal building, comprising a bar, servery and internal Gate 1, came into use. By the late summer, however, only fifteen regular flights per week were departing from Stansted: one Transeuropa Caravelle to Palma; one Britannia Airways Boeing 737 to the same place; a Tarom BAC 1-11 to (Rumania); a Viscount and a Herald of BAF to Jersey; seven Twin Otters of Jersey European also to Jersey; A BAF Viscount to Guernsey; a Boeing 737 of Orion Airways to Tenerife; and a Balkan Tu.154 to Constanta. All these international flights were of course under the heading of Inclusive Tours.

Unfortunately, Southern International went into receivership on 3 September 1981, and its

Seen on a very misty morning is Orion's Boeing 737-2T5 G-BJBJ .

Attractively-painted Viscount G-BAPE of Intra Airways at Stansted [via P. Kemp]

contracts were taken over by Air UK, which on 2 November recommenced its service from Stansted to Amsterdam, the first international scheduled sevice to use Stansted for about ten years. Twelve flights per week were scheduled, using Friendship aircraft, and permission was also obtained for Air UK to operate services to Paris and Brussels from Stansted. Also interested in the prospect of international services from Stansted was Jersey European, which wanted sanction to fly to Amsterdam, Paris and Brussels as well as to domestic destinations such as Belfast, Birmingham, Swansea and Liverpool.

Departing from the scene to a new home at Tees-Side airport in August 1981 was the CAA Fire Service Training School, which during the previous 22 years had trained 9000 airport firemen from no less than 82 countries. Aircraft used at the school included Lincoln and Shackleton, Hastings, Viscount, Prince, Britannia, Comet, DC-4, DC-7 and DC-8.

A new Stansted resident in the latter part of 1981 was Jointair, which used two Learjet 35A business jets. The winter IT season brought Aviaco DC-9s to Stansted on weekly flights to Palma (Majorca) and Tenerife and Balkan Tu.134s taking ski enthusiasts to Plovdiv, but Aviaco's Palma service was cancelled after only one flight due to very low passenger demand. From November, Air Atlantique Dakotas were much in evidence on mail flights to Liverpool, and the company had recently bought three aircraft from Eastern Airlines, creating a fleet of six of the type.

The new British Aerospace BAe 146 'whisper-jet' paid its first visit to Stansted on 13 October 1981 to give flights to members of the aviation press. This aircraft was the Series 100

The swing's the thing!

Heavylift's Conroy converted 'Skymonster' CL-44 EI-BND demonstrates what oversized air cargo is all about, as one of a pair of Bell 212 helicopters (minus rotors) is loaded aboard the freighter for the long trip to Australia.

G-SSSH, the prototype BAe 146, demonstrated to journalists at Stansted. [BAe]

prototype, G-SSSH, which had only taken to the air at Hatfield for the first time on 3 September, and it created a great deal of interest at Stansted, not least because of its very low noise level.

A final decision at last?

For Stansted airport, by far the most significant and far-reaching event of 1981 was the public enquiry which opened on 27 September into the proposed large-scale expansion of Stansted to form London's third airport. This enquiry, under the chairmanship of Graham Eyre QC, was held not at Charrington House as originally planned but in a conference room specially built at Quendon Hall at a cost of £113,000. In essence, the question was whether to allow the development of Stansted in two stages into an airport which eventually could handle 50 million passengers, the first stage, for completion in 1990, taking capacity to 15 million passengers per annum. The main alternatives to such expansion of Stansted were a fifth terminal at Heathrow, a new airport at Maplin Sands, expansion of regional airports or the conversion of an un-named RAF airfield. Lionel Read QC, for BAA, said that it was *"...Stansted or nothing"*, and the TGWU and other trade unions expressed their support. BAA's Chairman, Norman Payne, remarked that if expansion was

not allowed, the effect would be to restrict the number of potential passengers, thus pushing up air fares. However, Graham Eyre QC remarked on 7 January 1982 that the evidence provided by the Ministry of Aviation was most unsatisfactory, and new surveys of the effect of the proposed development would have to be prepared, as insufficient information on the loss of land to housing and industry was available.

Bad weather in December 1981 caused five aircraft to divert to Stansted, even though BAA refused to handle them due to an alleged lack of parking space. One, OD-AFU of Middle East Airlines, resorted to the desperate measure of declaring a fuel-state emergency in order to land.

Heavylift remained busy, carrying a number of awkward loads to far-flung places. Typical were the Skyvan of the Omani Air Force which G-BEPS brought to Bournemouth (Hurn) in November 1981 for repairs by Airwork; the Indian Air Force B-24 which arrived from Bangalore in one of the Belfasts before being trucked to Blackbushe for the Arnold collection in May 1982; and two Puma helicopters which flew in from Westland's at Yeovil to be de-rigged and loaded on a Belfast for export. By this time, Heavylift personnel were using computer-generated drawings for load planning purposes, ensuring that each item could be accommodated,

Airport safety equipment always has to be of the highest order - here is fire engine No.3, a Javelin.

A Convair 580 of Norfly.

even if the clearance was down to a few millimetres! Each Belfast had been 'hand-built' by Shorts, and thus had slightly different fuselage internal dimensions, allowing some aircraft to carry larger loads than others. The third Belfast, G-BFYU, entered service in 1982 and was employed on ferrying parts of the Boeing 767 aircraft from Naples to Seattle. In addition, major components of BAC 1-11 aircraft were carried in the Belfasts from Hurn to Rumania for assembly at the start of the ROMBAC programme.

Hijack!

By far the most exciting event at Stansted for many years was the arrival of the hijacked Air Tanzanian Boeing 737, 5H-ATC, on 27 February 1982. Soon after leaving Mwanza in Tanzania for Dar-es-Salaam as flight TC206 at 12.35 on the previous day, the aircraft had been taken over by members of the Tanzanian Youth Democracy Movement who demanded that the flight should divert to Nairobi. After four hours there the 737 took off for Jeddah in Saudi Arabia, where it landed at 03.00 on 27 February. With fuel tanks topped up, it left for Athens. From there the 737 took off at 09.40 and flew towards England, and when it was near Paris at 13.45 (local time) controllers at Stansted were advised. It touched down at 14.31 and was parked near the terminal building, and for the hostages a long wait began. Two Scout helicopters of the Army Air Corps

arrived, no doubt bringing personnel who would be involved in any action to free the hostages. The airport was closed to almost all traffic until such time as the problem could be resolved, and at 18.55 the Boeing was taxied nearer to the terminal. During Sunday 28 February the hostages were gradually released and at 16.22 the terrorists surrendered. The Tanzanian aircraft remained at Stansted until 3 March, when it was released to return home. Members of the international media had arrived in force at Stansted in the knowledge that the aircraft would land there, and were accommodated in the terminal building, which the hijackers then threatened to blow up. The pressmen then had to be hurriedly evacuated! On 17 September 1982, the leader of the hijackers, Moussa Membar, and four others were jailed for up to eight years.

Jersey Eurpopean was awarded a licence early in 1982 to fly a scheduled service from Stansted to Brussels, and opened the route on 3 May, using a Twin Otter which operated the night mail flights from Southend.

A railway strike in February 1982 created extra work for Instone Air Line and to the airlines which operated night mail flights - Eastern, Air Ecosse and Jersey European. DC-3s of Air Atlantique, Viscounts and Heralds of British Air Ferries and HS748s of Dan-Air were used to supplement the regular mail flights, producing a temporary increase in activity at Stansted.

Reproduced from a textured photograph, this apparently grainy image is of the Air Tanzania Boeing 737 5H-ATC that was hijacked by members of the Tanzanian Youth Democracy Movement to Nairobi. The hijacking eventually reached Stansted and a happy conclusion with the surrender of the terrorists.
[via P. Kemp]

THE STANSTED EXPERIENCE

High above the clouds is seen Fordair's out-of-sequence registered BAC-111 G-BFMC [Ford Motor Co. Ltd.]

Spring 1982 saw the beginning of the summer IT season, with Britannia Airways 737s and Spantax and Aviaco DC-9s flying to Palma weekly, Orion Airways 737s to Tenerife (soon cancelled due to lack of support), and JAT to Pula in Yugoslavia each week. One local IT operator, Classic Holidays of Sawbridgeworth, remarked in its summer brochure that *"...departures are exclusively from Stansted airport because we are a local company... ...and further, and much more importantly, Stansted airport is easily accessible, friendly, and offers the travelling public all possible facilities."* Another operator, Thomas Cook, predicted that Stansted would soon become the most popular departure airport for travellers living in East Anglia, north Kent and the south-east Midlands. Largely as a result of this increased IT traffic and transatlantic charter flights to Canada by Wardair, the airport's income rose by 21% in that year. Inbound charters were once again from Scandinavian countries, and included Norfly from Bergen, Busy Bee, Maersk and Linjeflyg.

Interesting aircraft pasing through Stansted during March 1982 included two DHC Buffalos bound for the Egyptian Air Force and BAC 1-11 551 of the Omani Air Force.

Aviation Traders, again a recipient of the Queen's Award for Export Achievement, was heavily involved at this time in dismantling a number of ex-Pan American Boeing 707s and the refurbishment and resale of others. In addition, three Airbuses formerly used by the sadly-missed Laker Airways were delivered at the end of May, while an ex-Laker DC-10 left for Boston after being sold.

A new company which began operating from Stansted in the spring of 1982 was Kondair, which took delivery of a Trislander on 1 March. Another new name appeared at Stansted in May 1982 when Inter-City Airlines began to take part in the ever-growing number of nightly newspaper flights, using a Viscount. Also present was American Overseas Airlines, which operated several flights to New York on behalf of American Express.

The public enquiry continues..........

Speaking on 13 May 1982, the 115th day of the enquiry at Quendon Hall, David Lloyd, representing four organisations concerned with heritage, gave the opinion that thousands of historic buidings would be threatened by the proposed development of Stansted. At least 107 listed buildings would be severely affected if not demolished if growth to the maximum proposed was permitted. If housing for airport workers was built at Harlow, the town would become an unacceptable sprawl four to five miles (six to eight km.) long [about twice its then size — author]. The character of Old Harlow and of Thaxted would be adversely affected by road traffic generated by the airport, he said, and housing associated with the airport could even put pressure on the centre of Cambridge. Pursuing a theme already mentioned, the Country Landowners' Association reiterated on 23 June that much more farmland would be lost to urbanisation than official estimates stated. There was also a good deal of concern among MPs, over a hundred of whom tabled a Parliamentary motion on 30 June opposing large-scale development of Stansted, remarking that *"...expansion would produce unjustifiable urban growth and congestion in north-west Essex and east Hertfordshire."* Uttlesford District Council, meanwhile, had become the main promoter of a proposed Terminal 5 at Heathrow instead of the development of Stansted and had submitted a planning application for a new sewage treatment works near the M4 motorway at Colnbrook. This was, however, firmly rejected by Buckinghamshire County Council on 30 July 1982.

Sunrise Airlines, just formed at Stansted, opened an IT service to Orlando in Florida on 29 July 1982, using a Boeing 707 hurriedly chartered from Sabena. The second trip a week later, however, was poorly patronised, and the few passengers were transferred to other airlines. Sunrise thus flew only one trip! Air Express International began a series of weekly scheduled cargo flights to New York on 18 July, for which two CL-44s were used, and these flights proved very successful. Inbound, Denver-based travel club Ports of Call started a series of charter flights and used Aviation Tarders to maintain their aircraft while at Stansted.

On 5 September an accident which could have been fatal occured at Stansted when Intercontinental Nigeria DC-8 RP-C830, flying in very bad visibility, hit the tailplane of Flying Tigers DC-8 N786FT, which was awaiting loading in the cargo area. Originating at Lagos and carrying 57 passengers and ten crew, the Intercontinental aircraft sustained damage to a wing and flap and diverted to Manchester for an emergency landing. There it was impounded by the CAA for non-payment of fees and some passengers were arrested for passport and drugs offences! Aviation Traders repaired the tail of the Flying Tigers aircraft, which left on 2 October. The aircraft had been the first of a series of bloodstock charter flights arranged by Instone, which had secured an ad hoc licence and planned to wet-lease DC-8s from Flying Tigers.

September 1982 also saw the first visit to Stansted of an Il.76, which stayed over the night of 12/13th. The aircraft, YI-AKX of Iraqi Airways, had come to collect a cargo of horses. Stansted's own freight airline, Heavylift, continued to expand, and took delivery of the less-than-pretty CL-44 'Skymonster' EI-BND from Southend on 5 November 1982. This aircraft entered service a week later by carrying Ford spares from Cologne to Liverpool. The

Falklands War saw the Belfasts flying Ministry of Defence material to Ascension Island for onward shipment to Port Stanley, the irony of which was not lost on the Royal Air Force! Other aircraft in the fleet were kept busy carrying outsize and awkward loads to many places worldwide.

Instone was also still very active, and one of their two Bristol Freighters was usually detached to Lydd Airport for trips to Rotterdam and other European cities not too far distant. Instone continued to charter aircraft from Flying Tigers for long-distance work, and in April for a charter to Australia a Boeing 747 was used for the first time.

At the public enquiry, BAA admitted on 15 December that it was concerned by the strength of opposition in Parliament, particularly by 24 MPs who supported the North of England Regional Consortium, which was pressing for development of eight regional airports instead of Stansted. A further 200 MPs of all parties were giving support to this proposition.

On 20 January 1983 a second Il.76 visited Stansted, this one (YI-ALR) in a mixture of Iraqi Air Force and Iraqi Airways markings.

Rapidly-expanding Air UK took delivery of its first Short SD3-30, G-BKDN, on 10 April 1983 and placed it into service on the Amsterdam and Humberside routes. Further deliveries of 3-30s then enabled the fleet of Bandeirantes to be reduced to five, two of which were chartered from Air Ecosse. By the autumn, Air UK's own Bandeirantes had all been disposed of and further examples were leased in to maintain services.

British Airways entered the fray at the public enquiry on 17 May 1983 by claiming that official forecasts of the growth of air travel supported its opinion that Stansted would become an expensive 'white elephant' if developed as London's third airport. Instead, Terminal 5 at Heathrow should be built. With this in use and existing terminal facilites at Heathrow, Gatwick, Luton and

Goodyear airship N2A Europa at its temporary mooring mast on the airport, complete with Landrover escort!

On finals: the space-shuttle Columbia on its Boeing 747 parent, NASA 905, about to touch down at Stansted [Peter Smith]

Stansted all able to handle small increases in passenger throughput, British Airways considered that London's requirements could be coped with until beyond the year 2000.

Boeing 707s continued to be the main pre-occupation of Aviation Traders in 1983, enlivened by an occasional civilian Hercules or by Viscounts, two of which, Turkish Air Force 430 and 431, arrived on 25 May for attention.

Air Malta Boeing 737s began making transit stops on their way from Leeds to Malta on 9 May, but the most significant new user of Stansted was Maof Airlines, an Israeli concern which had been using Luton as a UK terminal. From the end of June 1983, up to five flights per week by Maof's Boeing 707s or 720s were routed to Stansted, causing a considerable increase in security arrangements due to the airline's nationality, but it was expected that about 50,000 extra passengers would be handled at Stansted during the first year. A second Israeli concern, Arkia, began to use Stansted on 15 August for a short series of charters. Charter flights involving Scandinavian airlines continued and by now were often flown by more modern Airbus A.300 aircraft.

Arrival of the Space Shuttle

A once-in-a-lifetime event at Stansted was the visit on Saturday 5 June 1983 of the NASA Space Shuttle *'Enterprise'*, carried on the back of its Boeing 747-100 transporter, N905NA/NASA905. An estimated 750,000 people took the opportunity of inspecting the Shuttle at close quarters or as it arrived at the airport, and the nearby M11 motorway was almost clogged. To bring well-heeled spectators to Stansted in comfort, a helicopter service operated every few minutes from Harlow Heliport! The Shuttle stayed at Stansted until Monday before taking off for the United States via Keflavik (Iceland), making overshoots at Birmingham, Manchester, Prestwick and Glasgow on the way. In honour of the event, Air UK gave the name 'Enterprise' to Shorts SD3-30 G-BKDN.

Coincident with the visit of the Space Shuttle was a fuel strike at Luton, which caused large numbers of aircraft to be diverted to Stansted. Most of the regular Luton operators — Britannia, Monarch, Dan-Air, Orion and Air Malta — were thus seen at Stansted, and more executive aircraft than usual made visits. Cargo flights from Algeria were now quite commonplace, bringing Hercules

The Space Shuttle parked at Stansted during its once-in-a-lifetime visit.

Genair - based at Humberside Airport - started flying into Stansted in the autumn of 1983. Their Shorts 360 B-BKAT is seen in joint Genair/BCAL Commuter titling.
[Genair]

STANSTED SHORTS!

Also in 1983 a pair of Shorts 360s were painted in 'post office red' and Royal Mail livery for use on Datapost flights, one aircraft being used on the busy Stansted - Manchester night service. Here is G-RMSS on charter from Air Ecosse.
[Royal Mail]

Jersey Eurpoean was also a user of Stansted, their SD3-30 G-BJUK in evidence one sunny afternoon.
[Simon Peters]

and An.12 aircraft of Algerian Airlines to Stansted with increasing frequency. Their cargo was fruit, and also in that business was Zakani Aviation, which sent several Boeing 707s from Cyprus with loads of grapes. Most unusual visitors were Goodyear airship N2A, which arrived from Calais on 28 June to fly private guests around the locality, and Junkers Ju.52 N9012P, which flew in from Egelsbach, Germany, on 27 August on its way to Leicester.

The hangar previously used by CSE Aviation was taken over in the summer of 1983 by Inflite Aviation, a small concern devoted to maintenance of and modifications to corporate aircraft such as Gulfstreams and Citations and also light aircraft. Having used Stansted extensively for training by

two Apache aircraft, Thurston Aviation, which had become established at Stansted four years previously, was now expanding its air taxi and corporate aircraft handling operations. On 7 November there was echoes with the past when the RAF Museum took delivery of a Boeing B-17, N5237V, at the end of its final flight. The Flying Fortress was then dismantled and carried by road to the RAF Museum at Hendon, its engines going to Duxford for future use on the airworthy aircraft, 'Sally B'.

Highly important was the opening in August 1983 by Air UK of its service from Stansted to Paris, operated at first twice daily by Bandeirante aircraft. Another new service in the autumn of 1983 was opened by Genair, which began flying

Transatlantic charter passengers disembark from the rear door of Worldways DC-8 C-FCPO

to Humberside on 24 October. Leaving Stansted early in the morning, the flight allowed passengers to connect with flights from Humberside to Teesside, Glasgow, Belfast, Blackpool, Copenhagen and the Isle of Man. The return trip was timed to land at Stansted during the evening. On the other hand, Jersey European closed its Brussels route on 17 December 1983, concentrating resources on the Channel Islands services and on the nightly mail service to East Midlands and Liverpool. Permission to fly the Brussels route was then transferred to Air UK.

During November 1983 Instone's decided not to continue to operate their two Bristol Freighters, both of which were then made ready for a possible long-term lease to a foreign company. Although some Instone personnel were made redundant, Instone Holdings continued to act as freight and animal transport brokers, using the considerable experience built up during the previous few years. In 1984, one of the Freighters returned to New Zealand, while operation of the other one was taken over by Air Atlantique, which put it back into the racehorse-carrying business. Air Atlantique then moved its operation to Stansted, where very often its Dakota aircraft were present, a significant link with the past. These venerable aircraft were often used to carry parties of aviation enthusiasts to air shows around the country.

New scheduled services and IT charters helped the upward trend to Stansted's prosperity. Air UK started the ball rolling by announcing that it had gained sufficient confidence to use Stansted as its major hub, good news indeed for the airport. Early in April 1984 the airline opened a route to Edinburgh, using F-27 Friendship aircraft on the twice-daily service. At the same time, the frequency of the Amsterdam route was increased to four per day, meaning that, with the Paris and Brussels services, there were at least eight Air UK departures per day from Stansted.

Heavylift continued to be active during 1984, hardly any part of the world not receiving a visit from the Belfasts or CL-44s. Helicopters were an important item of cargo carried, as was the Arianne third stage rocket which Heavylift took to Cayenne in French Guiana. On the engineering side, Aviation Traders remained busy.

Transatlantic services

Transatlantic charters were, due to the weakness of the pound, prolific that year. Among the airlines involved were Canadian airline Wardair, which operated two flights per week at Stansted, one from Rome to Toronto and the other to Toronto via Birmingham. The United States was represented by Capitol Airways, which flew a number of DC-8 trips; Davis Air, which operated a weekly service to Miami and Atlanta with DC-8s of Rich Air; and Air National, operating Boeing 747s chartered from other American concerns. Another airline, which wanted to use Stansted for transatlantic scheduled services, was People Express, with whom discussions took place during the year. On the other hand, Maof

A British Airways Concorde takes off from Stansted behind a Lockheed Tristar of American Trans Air, N709DA. [Stansted Airport Ltd.]

Airlines of Israel, one of the Stansted regulars, ceased flying during the year, with a consequent reduction in activity (and security) at Stansted. Charter flights from Norway and Sweden continued, and the first Boeing 767 to be seen at Stansted was operated by Braathens, though some airlines considered this type of aircraft too large and expensive to operate over comparatively short stages.

Development to go ahead!

The public enquiry into Stansted's development took 258 days, during which 38 tonnes of paper were used! On 10 December 1984 Graham Eyre QC published his report, recommending that outline planning permission should be granted for the development of Stansted airport to handle fifteen million passengers per annum, and gave his opinion that only Stansted could provide the capacity needed in the London area by the mid-1990s. Development of Stansted should from the outset allow for an ultimate capacity which could be handled by using the existing runway — 25 million passengers per year. Under no circumstances should a second runway ever be built. In the local area the economy would benefit, with Harlow taking most of the associated housing development, and Bishops Stortford a lesser amount. Any loss of agricultural land would be more than offset by the importance of the airport development. The report criticised Government policy, commenting that it was *"...characterised by ad hoc expediency, unacceptable and ill-judged procedures, ineptness, vacillation, uncertainty and ill-advised and precipitate judgements."*

However, the long fight was not over, as MPs of all parties opposed the recommendations of the report. 74 Members signed an Early Day Motion over the development and a heated debate in Parliament ensued. Essex County Council also attacked the report, its Chairman, Ron Williams,

stating on 17 December *"We have always made it quite clear that we wish to see limited growth at Stansted within the existing airport's limits, and the Inspector's proposals that it should be expanded to take 15 million and then 25 million passengers a year are wholly unacceptable to us. The right place for airport growth on this scale is Heathrow, and we shall now be urging the Government... ...to reject the proposal for major expansion at Stansted."* BAA dropped its opposition to Terminal 5 at Heathrow on 15 January 1985, and called for urgent discussions on the proposed Stansted development. Next day, however, the Labour shadow cabinet stated its opposition to Stansted, transport spokesman Gwynedd Dunwoody MP saying that Labour would urge a debate in the House of Commons.

By the end of January 1985, senior Cabinet ministers were hinting that the proposal to develop Stansted to take 15 million passengers per year would not be approved in Parliament. They believed that growth in air traffic in south-east England would have to be taken by Terminal 5 at Heathrow and by a second runway at Gatwick, with some expansion at Manchester airport. Alan Haselhurst MP (Con.), in whose Saffron Walden constituency Stansted airport was located, remarked on 30 January that there was a deep sense of injustice locally. It made sense, he felt, to improve the environment at Heathrow, and access to it, before spending large sums of money in the countryside. Other MPs supported these comments.

To determine the strength of feeling among local residents, British Airways commissioned a Gallup Poll in May 1985. In the Poll, four options were put forward — Option A (no expansion) produced 50% for and 48% against, but Option B (expansion to 5 million passengers) showed 68% in favour and 19% against. Option C (expansion to the size of Gatwick) brought forward 32% for and 64% against, while Option D (expansion to

Air UK's BAC 1-11 G-AXMU in an interim colour scheme.

Heathrow size) produced, not surprisingly, only 13% for and 84% against. The first hint of financial compensation was given on 21 June 1985 by Michael Spicer MP, Under Secretary of State at the Dept. of Trade, who said that the Government might make an offer to residents adversely affected by the development.

During the financial year 1984/85, 547,000 passengers were handled at Stansted, an increase of 53% over the previous year, giving Stansted the title 'Fastest-growing airport' for the third successive year. The 40,000 passengers who flew on charters to the United States, ten times as many as the previous year, clearly contributed to this success. Air UK continued to expand its services from Stansted, although the Edinburgh service was reduced at the end of the 1985 summer. A route to Dusseldorf was opened but did not survive beyond October. Ever-increasing demand on the Paris and Amsterdam routes led to the introduction of Friendship aircraft to serve

these destinations, and in April 1985 afternoon flights to Amsterdam were further uprated when jet aircraft, including Fellowships, were introduced.

Charter flights continued to help Stansted's movement figures and passenger throughput in 1985, with Tristars of American Trans Air, Wardair's Boeing 747s and DC-10s and Worldways between them operating several flights each week. IT charters to the Mediterranean area from Stansted were, however, somewhat reduced in number due to lower package-holiday bookings. Prominent on the IT flights were the BAC 1-11s and Boeing 727-200s of Dan-Air, an airline becoming known among the tour operators for its 'value for money' approach.

Air Atlantique, a concern which had not been resident at Stansted for very long, left for a new base at Coventry at the end of 1985 after selling some of its mail-carrying contracts and the three

Dan-Air's 1-11 G-AXCK on the apron at Stansted. Behind can just be seen a Trident of British Airways on a training schedule.

Caravelle 108 SE-DEH of Transwede sparkles in the evening sunlight as it taxies past the Control Tower in September 1986. In the background can be seen the original Fordair hangar with a 1-11 nosing into it.
[D. Mason]

Dakotas which had been used on them to Air Luton earlier in the year. The one and only Bristol Freighter was, however, retained, and was seen at Stansted from time to time. The Algerian Government fleet of Hercules and An.12 aircraft continued to visit Stansted frequently to deliver fruit. Much less common was a CASA 212 of the Chilean Navy, which called in on 17 April 1985 on its way to Madrid and returned on 5 July.

Work begins on the new airport

1985 was the year in which Stansted's future as a major airport was finally settled. Nicholas Ridley, the Transport Secretary, published a White Paper entitled *'Airports Policy'* on 5 June, approving at long last the development of Stansted to handle 8 million passengers per year, rising to an eventual figure of 15 million. Prominent architect Sir Norman Foster was commissioned to design the terminal building and other new facilities, and to provide rapid transport from and to the London area British Rail was asked to undertake a study of possible rail links. Airlines, however, expressed reluctance to take advantage of the facilities which would be created. The most prominent user of Gatwick airport for scheduled services, British Caledonian, complained that if any airlines would be compelled to move to Stansted it should be those in the IT business. Britannia Airways and Monarch Airlines were also opposed to this idea, Monarch revealing that journeys to Stansted would take about 30 minutes longer and up to £20 extra per passenger would have to be charged on holidays to the Mediterranean area.

Michael Spicer MP, by now the Minister for Aviation, announced in Parliament on 10 March 1986 that a £290 million investment in a new terminal building had been sanctioned, subject to detailed planning approval from Uttlesford District Council, which, he noted, had opposed the development until it had been approved by Parliament. After a remarkably short planning stage, Michael Spicer formally inaugurated the project on site on 15 April 1986. Detailed plans of the terminal building were disclosed by BAA at the end of May, when the architect, Norman Foster, said *"The BAA brief was for an efficient, cost-effective and joyful building. Calm, clarity and convenience are the key words."* Norman Payne, Chairman of the BAA, remarked that the building would be built at no cost to the taxpayer. The next five years were to see, on the south-eastern side of the runway, considerable

Michael Spicer MP, the Minister for Aviation (right) and Alan Munds of the BAA inaugurating work on the new terminal on 15 April 1986.
[Stansted Airport Ltd.]

A visitor to Stansted was Cubana Il-76 CU-T1258 [D. Mason]

upheaval, involving the demolition of existing hangars and dozens of small buildings, many of them dating from USAAF days, and provision of access roads before construction of the planned buildings could begin. To cope with additional business in the short term, small-scale improvements and extensions were put in hand in the existing terminal building.

The historic announcement was good news for a number of airlines, particularly Air UK, which reported that it hoped to be Stansted's principal scheduled service operator for many years to come. People Express, still intent on using Stansted as its terminal, increased the pressure on both Governments to award an operating licence for a daily service from Newark, New Jersey. Rapidly growing more active on the cargo area was Federal Express, which from 15 June 1985 was sending parcel-carrying Boeing 727-200s across the Atlantic five nights every week, carrying on to Brussels after an hour's stop. By October the business had outgrown the Boeing 727, and DC-10s were introduced for some flights. A local concern, Tal-Air, was contracted to carry Stansted-generated freight to Brussels, for which it used Bandeirante aircraft. Other Tal-Air aircraft, King Air and BAe125, were being used on casualty flights and

private charters within Europe. New to Stansted in September 1985 was Blades Helicopters, which began to use a Gazelle helicopter on charter work in the racing industry as well as some tuition.

Air UK, still growing, recommenced flying the Guernsey route in the spring of 1986, offering the option of a through Guernsey - Stansted - Brussels flight. Other through routes operated in 1986 included Stansted - Leeds/Bradford - Belfast and Leeds - Stansted - Paris, on which Friendships were used. Fares claimed to be the lowest in Britain were available on a Friendship which positioned from Stansted to Southampton on summer Saturday mornings and returned on Sunday evenings: £10 APEX return! Frankfurt was added to Air UK's destination lists during the year and soon produced good load factors.

The sale of Tradewinds to the Chairman of Tal-Air in March 1986 brought the former airline to Stansted in readiness for the commencement of twice-weekly flights to Chicago on 17 May as well as ad-hoc charters. The Saturday trips proved very successful, but the Wednesday flight had much lower load factors and was cancelled in July, although it was reinstated two months later. Tal-Air provided ground services to Tradewinds, at the same time maintaining the nightly flights to

A view of construction of the rapid transit tunnel for the link between the new terminal and it's satellites.

Meeting of the mighty at Stansted —Boeing 747 C-FDJC of Wardair and N637US of Northwest Orient on charter flights.
[Stansted Airport Ltd.]

Brussels. By September Tal-Air was also operating on behalf of United Parcels Service by flying parcels from Cologne to Stansted for onward despatch.

Transatlantic charters flown by US airlines suffered a serious reduction in 1986 due to worries about terrorism, the complete American Trans Air programme being being cancelled. Inbound charters from Scandinavian countries were not affected in that way, however, and Kar-Air began to use DC-10s on their flights. Scanair and Transwede were also prominent.

An unusual visitor to Stansted on 28 June 1986 was a 747 of Northwest Orient, N637US, which was present for two days to take part in an air display at North Weald by flying in formation with a Dakota painted in Northwest colours. During the latter part of the year a DHC-7 aircraft of Brymon Airways carried out a number of flights at Stansted so that the CAA to evaluate the 'steep approach' ILS which was to be installed at the new London City Airport and at Plymouth.

Administratively, Stansted Airport changed hands on 1 August 1986, when Britsh Airports Authority became a Limited Company, BAA plc, which now owned the airport through a subsidiary, Stansted Airport Ltd. Recently-knighted Sir Norman Payne told a meeting of airline representatives in London on 20 January 1987 *"I can promise you that the £290 million development* [at Stansted] *will provide an exciting and innovative new terminal building."* He then implied that some airlines might be compelled to move from Heathrow and Gatwick to Stansted. This idea began to have some substance when several IT flights were diverted from Gatwick that summer due to a lack of night-time 'slots'. Typical of these was an Air Europe flight which arrived from Faro in Portugal in the early hours of 28 August carrying passengers who became even more disgruntled when they found themselves aboard a coach to take them to Gatwick to collect their cars.

Business continued to grow during 1987, by

Stansted's ultra-modern new passenger terminal building under construction. The numerous steel 'trees' supporting the roof are very noticable.

The framework of Enterprise House under construction - before the application of the distinctive tinted green glass covering.

which time twelve destination airports were being served, eleven of them by Air UK, which flew to Aberdeen, Amsterdam, Belfast, Brussels, Edinburgh, Frankfurt, Guernsey, Jersey, Leeds/Bradford, Paris and Southampton, while Jersey European served Dinard and paralleled Air UK's Jersey and Guernsey flights. A newcomer, Stansted Airlines, applied in January 1987 for a licence to operate a scheduled service to Dublin from 1 June, using Herald aircraft. Confusingly-named Air Stansted also wished to serve Dublin, as well as Belfast Harbour and Belfast (Aldergrove). Another airline hoping to begin flying from Stansted was Highland Express, which planned three flights per week to the United States and one to Canada, using 500-seat Boeing 747s and, for a limited period, charging £118 for a one-way ticket. The first Highland Express aircraft arrived at Stansted on 21 June and began operating to Newark, New Jersey, via Prestwick nine days later. Sad to say, this airline lasted but a very short time before going into the hands of a receiver on 1 December 1987.

Incoming schedules for the summer included a service from Amsterdam by NLM Cityhopper and Air UK jointly using Friendships and Air France from Paris with new Saab 340s. Both these routes were opened on 30 March. Outgoing IT charter flights were still increasing in number, and a newcomer to this field in 1987 was Air Atlantis, which began a summer series of flights to Faro in Portugal on 1 May. Also becoming prominent was Air Malta, which used leased Boeing 727s. Cargo business also continued to develop, a newcomer being Air Cologne, which began a nightly service into Stansted using DC-9 aircraft of SAS, its parent company. On the other hand, United Parcel Service left Stansted in late 1987 in favour of Southend for logistic reasons. Notable in December 1987 were two cargo flights into Stansted by Boeing 747s of Korean Airlines.

Long-established Aviation Traders (Engineering) Ltd. was taken over from Aer Lingus at the end of March 1987 by Cambridge-based Qualitair Aviation (Holdings) Ltd. The new owners at once gave the news that major new facilities envisaged earlier by Aviation Traders were to be built at Stansted at a cost of £17 million to cope with the expanding business, and up to 600 more staff would be employed. Prominent would be a new hangar to accommodate two Boeing 747s or up to ten 737s, and on this building work began without delay. The company's name was changed on 14 August 1987 to Qualitair Aviation Ltd.

An event of a nature rarely seen at Stansted took place on 28 April 1987 when a number of aircraft powered by Rolls-Royce engines were displayed to prospective shareholders in the company. Viewed from a specially-erected marquee on the airfield side of the fence was a tantalising series of exhibits chosen to illustrate the seventy-year involvement of Rolls-Royce in the aircraft industry. From the Shuttleworth Collection at Old Warden came Hawker Hind K5414, parked alongside Hurricane PZ865 of the Battle of Britain Memorial Flight, which also sent

A Korean Airlines Cargo Boeing 747F being loaded.

Making a fly-by down the length of the runway at Stansted for the launch of the Rolls-Royce Prospectus was Boeing 747-338 VH-EBX of the Australian airline QANTAS.

Spitfire Vb AB910, Lancaster PA474 and Devon VP981. The Royal Navy's Historic Aircraft Flight provided Firefly AS.5 WB271, while more modern Fleet Air Arm aircraft on show were a Sea King and a Lynx. Aircraft of the Royal Air Force on the apron that day were a Jaguar, a Tornado, a Buccaneer, a Hawk, two Harriers and, last but by no means least, the sole remaining airworthy Vulcan, XH558, from Waddington. Civilian aircraft included a Gulfstream 2, a BAe 125, a Boeing 757, a BAC 1-11, a Friendship and a Viscount. For an hour the airport was closed to allow a fly-past of some of these aircraft to take place, supplemented by Concord G-BOAE, a British Airways Tristar and a Boeing 747-300 of Qantas.

To enable the airline to become involved in the IT market, Air UK decided in 1987 to form a subsidiary company, Air UK (Leisure) Ltd., which would begin operations from a Stansted base early the following year. It would be equipped with Boeing 737 aircraft, and planned to carry 120,000 passengers in its first year of operation, rising rapidly up to 400,000 in the fourth year. The parent company transferred its operations department from Norwich to Stansted during November 1987 in order to be closer to the action.

Traffic to Ireland was by 1988 increasing, prompting Aer Lingus to begin a daily service from Stansted to Dublin on 1 March, with an introductory single fare of £29. Significant expansion by Air UK meant that from 27 March a twice-daily schedule to Glasgow came into being, one flight being flown via Edinburgh, while frequency on the Paris service was stepped up to four flights each day. On the Brussels route Friendships replaced the much smaller SD3-60s. New on the Stansted scene was recently-formed Titan Airways, which took delivery of a Bandeirante and a Cessna Titan for passenger and freight charter work, and was considering operating scheduled services to European destinations, using a Dornier 228. This type was already in use by Suckling Airways on its Amsterdam service, which had been forced out of Ipswich due to the condition of the grass runway there and was by June using Stansted temporarily. On 18 July, however, Suckling moved to a new base at Cambridge.

Air UK Leisure opened its long-awaited IT services on 30 April 1988, by which time twelve or more tour operators had booked seats for the season. First aircraft away was Boeing 737-200 G-BNZT, which left Stansted for Jersey. Air UK Leisure then applied for permission to operate scheduled services to a number of holiday destinations in Spain, Portugal and the Canary Islands. The first new Boeing 737-400 aircraft for the airline, G-UKLA, was delivered from the

Suckling Airways used Stansted for its scheduled services to Amsterdam and Manchester for a time before settling at Cambridge. The airline's only aircraft at the time was Dornier 228 G-BMMR. [D. Mason]

G-UKLB 'Flagship St Francis' was one of Air UK Leisure's Boeing 737-4YOs, used exclusively for IT charter work. [D. Mason]

makers via Frobisher Bay and East Midlands in October 1988. Air UK Leisure was the first airline outside the United States to use this model.

Developments on the cargo area in 1988 included the demise of Air Cologne and the take-over of its customers by TNT, which introduced a BAe.146 on four flights to Nuremberg per week. This activity lasted only until 20 April before TNT left Stansted. Long-term resident Heavylift was still very much in evidence, although cargo activity at Stansted increased when Cathay Pacific began to operate twice-weekly cargo flights from Hong Kong on 4 May, the Boeing 747 calling at Dubai, Abu Dhabi and Frankfurt on the way. Tradewinds and Thurston Aviation, however, both found themselves in financial difficulty and came under administration in October, although Tradewinds was back in business after a few weeks, armed with a contract to fly on behalf of Royal Jordanian Airlines. A new company, Westair, began operating a Herald aircraft in November on cargo charter work.

Transatlantic services flown to and from Stansted in 1988 included flights to Montreal, Vancouver and Toronto by Air Transat to Florida and the Dominican Republic by Lion Air on behalf of Airtours, and from New York by Trans International, which used DC-8 aircraft.

On 15 November 1988 a lady arriving from Amsterdam became Stansted's first one-millionth passenger in a twelve-month period. During financial year 1986/87 550,000 passengers had used the airport, but in the following twelve months this figure increased to 720,000 and was still rising rapidly. In the six months from April 1988 more passengers passed through Stansted's gates than in the whole of financial year 1987/88! Further improvements therefore had to be made to the passenger-handling facilities, even though the completely new terminal building could be seen rising from the ground on the other side of the airport!

Work on the new terminal building proceeded smoothly, and a three-week period ending on 19 August 1988 was given to archeologists searching for artefacts on the site of the short-term car park, where the tomb of a wealthy Roman landowner had been found. Coins, pottery, engraved gemstones and bronze pieces were found here, while the remains of nine round houses occupied by Celts between 75 and 25 BC were located where the main parking apron is now.

One of the new BAe.146 aircraft for Air UK, G-BNND, visited Stansted for the first time on 17 December 1988, the forerunner of many landings

Air UK's Fokker F.27-200 G-BDVS named 'Friendship Eric Gandar Dower' after the famous Aberdeen-based aviation pioneer.

*BAe.146 G-BNJI
before delivery to the
San Diego based
Pacific Southwest
Airlines.*

of the type, although it was introduced on Gatwick—Glasgow and Edinburgh routes before becoming common at Stansted. Air Bremen, a new German operator, opened a route from Bremen, Munster and Paderborn on 10 April 1989, using Saab 340 aircraft on three trips each weekday and one on Saturdays and Sundays.

Cargo centre opens

The first section of the new airport, Phase 1 of the cargo centre, was opened on 22 May 1989 by Lord Brabazon of Tara, the Minister of State for Aviation. Designed and built by J A Elliott Ltd. of Bishops Stortford at a cost of £4.5 million, this phase consisted of a bonded warehouse 9000 sq. metres (96,840 sq. ft.) in area, and was occupied by G H Stansted Ltd., Servisair and Federal Express. Eight stands capable of handling aircraft up to the size of a Boeing 747F were provided, and the capacity of the centre was 100,000 tonnes per year. To expedite cargo movement, an advanced computer-based customs clearance and documentation system is shared with Gatwick and Heathrow, enabling freight forwarders to

Airfreight and urgent package carrier Federal Express brought numerous aircraft to Stansted. Above is one of their 727 freighters N219FE ......whilst a slightly larger machine was this DC-10-30AF model, N305FE, seen here in August 1986. [D. Mason]

The huge 'Diamond' hangar seen from the air.

[FLS Aerospace]

track the location of their cargoes at any stage. Another operator, Iberia, soon began a nightly cargo service from Madrid and Barcelona using Boeing 727s. Federal Express consolidated its operation at Stansted and operated a morning service from Frankfurt, continuing to New York.

The 'diamond hangar' in service

Also opened in May 1989 was the diamond-shaped hangar, unique in this country, originally envisaged by Aviation Traders. Designed by Faulks Perry Culley & Rech, the £20 million building was erected by Costains, who had started work in June 1987. The double-triangle principle made the most cost-effective use of available land and had been based on the TWA hangar at Miami International Airport. By the time it was opened, the huge hangar was in the hands of Qualitair Aviation Ltd. Such was the impact of the building that it won both the Building and the Supreme prizes at the 1989 British Construction Industry Awards Ceremony, and it boasts the world's longest

curtain rail, which can be used to separate the two halves of the hangar! The first aircraft to enter the hangar was a Boeing 707 of ZAS. Later in the year, Qualitair was itself taken over by one of its shareholders, the Swedish FFV Group, who renamed the company FFV Aerotech Stansted.

Traffic continued to grow substantially during 1989, and it appeared that the two million passenger capacity of the old terminal would be reached before the new one was due to be ready. Charter flights were operated that summer to eight Caribbean destinations, three in Florida and to Hawaii, New York, Los Angeles, Toronto, Vancouver, Montreal, Malaysia and East Africa as well as many to European sun-spots.

Heavylift, meanwhile, was actively involved in the enormous clean-up operation after the

Inside the diamond hangar.

In the left background is a 747; Ryanair 737 EI-ACR recieves some attention to it's fin and rudder. In the foreground FLS staff carefully manouvre the fin of British Airways' 737-236 G-BGDE 'Bride of Manchester' in it's lifting frame. [FLS Aerospace]

Exxon Valdez oil tanker disaster off Alaska, carrying two pollution control boats in each Belfast aircraft from Brest in France to Anchorage. This operation was seen to justify Heavylift's foresightedness in acquiring the aircraft several years previously. A similar task was the uplifting from Bremen of arctic exploration equipment for carrying to Sonderstromfiord in Greenland.

Air UK Leisure continued to expand, and during a temporary grounding of all Boeing 737-300s and -400s due to the Kegworth air disaster chartered aircraft from other airlines to bridge the gap between capacity and demand. These aircraft were of many types, giving passengers the chance of flying in something different. By the time the airline's third 737-400 was placed in service it was claimed that Air UK Leisure's fleet was the youngest in the world, the average age being less than four months!

An airline which would quickly become a major force at Stansted, Ryanair, began in a small way on 30 May 1989, when it opened a BAC 1-11 service to Connaught (Knock) on three days per week. Before long it was competing with Aer Lingus on the Dublin route on the other three weekdays, the official policy of the Government of Ireland being to prevent Aer Lingus securing a monopoly on this route and to encourage Ryanair, or another airline, to take a share of the traffic. A complete surprise came in September 1989, however, when the Irish Government banned Aer Lingus from flying the Stansted route for a period of three years. Ryanair was thus able to consolidate its two routes to great advantage.

The winter of 1989/90 was a poor one for the holiday industry, and a number of tour operators retreated to their primary bases at Gatwick and Luton airports, leaving Stansted somewhat high and dry apart from the activities of Air UK, Ryanair and the Civil Aviation Flying Unit, which was as busy as ever.

Into the new decade!

At the beginning of the final decade of the twentieth century, considerable progress was being made with the development of Stansted Airport as a major part of the United Kingdom air travel scene. Construction of the new terminal building and associated facilities was well under way and the cargo area had already been opened for business. In anticipation of future traffic, the new 237-bedroom Stansted Harliquin hotel, later to become the Hilton National, built on land between the airport and the M11 motorway and close to the future long-term car park, came into use in July 1990.

FFV Aerotech remained busy on aircraft maintenance, and in February 1990 signed a contract with British Airways for overhaul and modifictaion work to five Boeing 747s. With the gradual reduction in numbers of Boeing 707s and DC-8s in service world-wide, FFV's activities now involved more 737s and 757s, a trend which would develop over the next few years.

An important addition to the growing cargo element of Stansted's business came early in 1990, when Russian airline Aeroflot announced its intention of operating weekly flights from Vladivostok, to where containerised freight would be shipped from countries in the Far East to be flown in Il.76 aircraft to Stansted. Two trial flights were made early in July from Moscow to collect a cargo of pesticides. When the service began, on 13 October, the destination was Tokyo, via Moscow, however. Other cargo airlines using Stansted's facilities continued to increase their business. New services included, from Cologne, a weekly trip by UPS with DC-8 aircraft, while using Boeing 747s, Federal Express opened a cargo service from Bangkok via Dubai and Frankfurt, calling at Stansted before leaving for New York.

TAT began flying a scheduled service to Stansted from Tours and Poitiers in France whilst Air UK introduced the BAe146 aircraft to the Amsterdam, Glasgow, Edinburgh and Guernsey routes from Stansted in the spring of 1990, leaving Friendships on the Brussels and Paris services. The airline had welcomed in 1989 an increase of 16% in the number of passengers it flew from or to Stansted. Another airline determined to develop its business at Stansted was Ryanair, which announced plans to introduce new routes in 1991, and even Aeroflot entered discussions with Stansted management about a

Ryanair's BAC 1-11 'The Spirit of Tipparary', EI-BSY.

THE STANSTED EXPERIENCE

Crossair's SAAB HB-AKP surrounded by Servisair ground handling equipment. [Dave Mason]

possible passenger route from Kiev to be opened in 1991. Air Bremen, however, disappeared from Stansted on 23 August 1990, and Proteus Air Services, operating a service to Dijon, experienced difficulties which stopped the service for a short time.

The first charter ever flown to East Germany took off from Stansted in August 1990 bound for Colditz Castle. Carrying 172 former prisoners and their friends, the aircraft used was a Boeing 737 of Air UK Leisure on a very different task from those it usually performed. Also from behind what was still then the 'Iron Curtain' were two Il.18 aircraft which brought 200 children from Chernobyl on their way to Tel Aviv, Stansted being used for refuelling.

Heavylift found the beginning of the nineties just as active a period as the previous decade. Twice each week, Heavylift's recently-acquired Boeing 707s were flying a freight service to Chicago for British Airways, and once weekly to Hong Kong. When not in use on these flights, the 707s were flown on ad hoc charters. The Belfasts and the 'SkyMonster', meanwhile, continued the well-established business of carrying heavy and/or outsize loads anywhere in the world, and in the spring of 1990 were involved in flying relief supplies to Sudan and Ethiopia, power station components to the United States, a collection of works of art from Geneva to Warsaw, blankets and tents to Iran and vehicles to Brunei. Very little work was outside Heavylift's scope!

By August 1990 167 scheduled flights were taking off from Stansted each week to 17 destinations, and 43,930 passengers were carried that month, an increase of 15% over the same month in 1989.

In January 1991 the long-awaited application for a daily service between Stansted and New York was submitted to the CAA by American Airlines, a route which would act as a 'seed-bed' service to encourage other airlines to make more use of the new facilities. Another application submitted that month was for routes by Jersey

European Airlines to serve Belfast, Newcastle and Munich, but these of course were much less contentious than the transatlantic proposal. Air UK also planned to introduce new services, connecting Stansted with Aberdeen, Dusseldorf, Florence, Frankfurt, Newcastle and Nice, all to use BAe.146 aircraft. Additional flights were added to Ryanair's Dublin route, and new services to Galway, Waterford, Knock, Kerry and Munich were planned by the Irish airline, which had decided to concentrate most of its services on Stansted.

The Gulf war had its effect on Stansted, which was specified as one of the airports designated to receive wounded troops on their way to hospitals of the North East Thames Regional Health Authority, a facility that was not required.

Aeroflot's cargo service into Stansted developed rapidly, and brought an example of the huge An.124 (CCCP-82027) from Singapore via Luxembourg on 7 February 1991. A sister aircraft appeared on 11 February, and examples of other Russian aircraft, the Il.76, Tu.134 and Tu.154 were by now quite common at Stansted.

Soon to be opened, the new terminal building was the scene of a recording of the BBC TV programme 'Songs of Praise' on 20 January 1991. Fifteen hundred people from churches within an eight-mile radius of the airport took part, and a choir of 450 was drawn from the same sources. This service, which was regarded as a dedication, was probably the first time an airport had been used as the backdrop to the programme.

One of the UK's fast-expanding holiday tour companies, Airtours, was in the process of buying five McDonnell Douglas MD.83 aircraft with which to operate its own airline, and in February 1991 decided to base one of them at Stansted from April, with support personnel. Early in March crew training began, and on 15 March a promotional flight to Paris (Orly) took place. The planned Air UK and Ryanair routes opened in March, and added to them was a route to Basle flown by Crossair and a twice-daily service to Bordeaux by Air France.

Chapter Eight

Today and Tomorrow

Undoubtedly the most important event in the long and chequered history of Stansted Airport was the opening of the new terminal facilities by Her Majesty the Queen on 15 March 1991.

Fifteen hundred guests were present to welcome Her Majesty, who arrived by special train from London. In his speech, Sir Norman Payne, Chairman of BAA, said *"We don't build white elephants. We build the very best terminals in the world...[we are sure] that by next spring it will be 'all systems go'."* Unfortunately, only two days earlier BAA had had to announce a 33% fall in aircraft movements at Stansted compared with the same period in 1990. A flypast by several types of aircraft representing the history of aviation at Stansted had been planned, was cancelled due to the Gulf crisis, and so instead a single Harrier flew past and 'bowed' to the Royal party.

Work on the new building, designed by prominent architects Foster & Associates, had begun in the spring of 1986. In a nine-week period, about 1.5 million cubic metres (almost 2 million cubic yards) of soil had been excavated so that the building could be partly sunk into the ground to a depth of 12m. (39ft.) to reduce its impact on the environment. At the same time, work began on the construction of the new road system to allow direct access from the M11 motorway at Junction 8, a facility essential for the large numbers of vehicles delivering materials to the building site. Foundations for the terminal building were completed in February 1987 in

readiness for the erection of the steel frame. Consisting of 36 steel 'trees' 17m. (55'9") long by 3.5m. (11'6") square, the largest that could be transported from the manufacturing plant by road, the frame supports 121 roof canopies, each 18m. (59ft.) square weighing 14 tonnes. These domes are 23m. (75'6") above the undercroft floor, and the main concourse floor, which has its own free-standing concrete structure, was built only after the roof had been completed. All the frame members were bolted together at ground level, thus eliminating site welding operations. The building, measures 180m. (590ft.) square externally, giving a floor area of 32000 sq.m. (344320 sq.ft., about 8 acres or 3.25 hectares), which is approximately the size of Trafalgar Square. At its forecourt the terminal building is 15m. (49ft.) high, the same height as surrounding mature trees.

Four days after the opening ceremony, at 05.00 on 19 March, the travelling public began to use the building, and the first passengers to enter it, the Walker family from Great Yarmouth, were presented with a bottle of champagne before leaving for Malta. All passengers that day were given a commemorative envelope to mark the occasion. The first flight to depart from the new satellite was an Air UK BAe.146 which left at 07.20 for Glasgow, followed by a Boeing 737 of Air UK Leisure which took off for Malta and an Air UK BAe.146 for Amsterdam. Arriving, the first aircraft was an ATR.42 of Air France, which touched down at 07.40 from Paris.

For a passenger departing from Stansted, this is their first view of the Foster Associates terminal design. The spacious passenger drop-off zone is noticable, as is the huge 'trees' supporting the roof. [Simon Peters]

THE STANSTED EXPERIENCE

Construction work around the airport continued. On 19 February 1991 a new Training Centre for airport staff was opened in Blunt's Farmhouse, which had been bought by the BAA as far back as October 1980. In September 1990, renovation costing £130,000 had been put in hand there to create a conference room, lecture rooms, a lounge, a kitchen and other facilities. The airport's new seven-bay Fire Station, situated next to the Cargo Centre, was opened on 15 April 1991. Constructed by JT Design & Build of Bristol at a cost of £3.6 million, the new building replaced one on the opposite side of the runway which was too small to accommodate the increase in appliances and personnel required for the airport's growth. Provision was made to accommodate two Meteor and three Javelin foam tenders and 69 personnel in the new station. In March, a new Eastern Access Plan had been lodged with Uttlesford District Council, reflecting a need for an entrance to the airport capable of handling traffic volumes in the mid-1990s prior to opening of the new A120 road diversion.

As part of the Tidy Britain Group's "Get a grip on litter" campaign, staff volunteers carried out a major spring-cleaning task around the airport on 25 April 1991, a day before it was announced that a jury of international experts had selected the new Stansted terminal building to receive the prestigious Miles van der Rohe Pavilion Award for European architecture. The award was presented on 27 April to Managing Director of the airport, Eric Lomas, and architect Sir Norman Foster, at a ceremony at Barcelona.

During April 1991, the first full month after the opening of the terminal, over 85,000 passengers used it, an increase of 2% over April 1990 at a time when throughput at the other London airports was falling. Of the total, 56,000 passengers were on scheduled flights, an increase of no less than 60%! By May 1991, seven airlines (Air UK, Ryanair, Crossair, Air France, Proteus, Noble Air, and TAT) were operating 676 flights each week to 25 destinations in Europe, but so far no transatlantic service had developed. Thirteen of the destination airports were on Air UK routes, making this airline the main 'customer' of Stansted. Also very prominent was Ryanair, which was by now operating routes to five Irish destinations and across to Munich, almost 100 flights per week in all. The other routes were those of TAT to Tours and Poitiers, Noble Air to Istanbul, Proteus to Dijon, Crossair to Basle and Air France to Paris and Bordeaux. The

Above: Stansted's much-modified control tower complex, built from and around the wartime structure that was a 12779/41 design. [Author]

Left: In the original control tower, a controller gives a just-landed aircraft taxying instructions. On the rain-soaked apron on 26 January 1995 can be seen a Short 360, two light twins and a huge Antanov freighter. [Author]

Welcome to Stansted Airport

Passengers arriving or departing from the airport have access to supurb public transport facilities; there is a railway station within the terminal with excellent links to London.
[all Simon Peters]

upward trend continued in May, when 159,800 passengers arrived or departed, including 95,000 on the scheduled flights, an increase of nearly 150% since the same month in 1990. Charter traffic, however, suffered a fall of 7%.

A £2 million scheme to provide sound insulation in 600 houses in a corridor between Thaxted and Sawbridgeworth was introduced by Stansted Airport Ltd. in June 1991, well in advance of Government stipulations. Before the Dept. of Transport's closing date for grant applications, 31 May 1993, over 650 households applied, and work was completed in November 1994.

Activity at the airport continued to grow remarkably in the summer and autumn of 1991, and on 8 July British Rail opened the rail link to Cambridge, Peterborough and the Midlands and North of England to ease the flow of airport-related traffic. All records of passengers using scheduled services and the General Aviation terminal were broken in June, with 15% more passengers than in the previous June, and again in July, when the increase was 43%. The millionth passenger to use the new terminal building arrived on a Crossair BAe.146 flight from Basle on 13 September 1991, by which time the throughput had risen to over 200,000 per month. Winter schedules were now being planned, and included services to Maastricht by Air Exel three times daily from January 1992; Kristiansand by

Norsk Air from 28 October; Metz/Nancy by Luxair from early November 1991; Lille by Air France; Dijon by Proteus; Montpelier by Air Littoral twice a week from 30 November, Biarritz by the same airline on Saturdays, and Bucharest by Tarom. These flights would bring the average weekly number of scheduled movements at Stansted during the winter to 792 — 130 on average each weekday, 57 on Saturdays and 85 on Sundays. Even more significant was the announcement made by American Airlines on 21 August that it had decided to begin the long-awaited non-stop Chicago service on 16 June 1992, using Boeing 767 aircraft. A little later, the Stansted authorities revealed that they were in touch with their counterparts at Nashville, Tennessee, with a view to arranging a direct service between the two airports. Urging the US Government to support the proposal was Congressman Bob Clement, who visited London early in the New Year.

New Instrument Landing System equipment was brought into use on 20 September 1991, allowing Category 2/3 operations and permitting aircraft to make an approach in visibility as low as 50 metres (164 feet). Stansted now met British Airways' recently-introduced standards for operation of the Boeing 747-400 and 767 types, prior to which the minimum visibility for ILS operations at Stansted had been 800 metres (2624 feet), with a cloudbase of 61m. (200ft.).

THE STANSTED EXPERIENCE

Jointly operated by Heavylift and Volga Dnieper, this Antanov An.124 dwarfs everything surrounding it. [D Mason]

Heavylift continued to expand its almost-unique services during the early 1990s by entering a joint-venture agreement with Volga-Dnieper of Ulyanovsk in the former Soviet Union. In September 1991 the first enormous An.124 Russlan, CCCP-82042, arrived for the venture, and was painted in Heavylift colours. This aircraft was soon joined by a second example, and the venture came into the public eye when a first load of beef flown to Moscow was held up there due to fears of BSE, but this matter was soon resolved.

In recognition of the civil engineering and building projects which had taken place, Stansted Airport won the British Construction Industry Supreme Award on 24 October 1991. The citation stated that Stansted was *"....an object lesson in the successful marriage of architectural and engineering design with construction and management skills of the highest order."* Within two weeks, Stansted Airport was honoured at the CBI Conference when Michael Heseltine MP presented the Business & Industry Committment to the Environment Premier Award to Eric Lomas, Managing Director of Stansted Airport Ltd. For marketing the advantages of the new terminal and the services available to travellers, the airport authorities had used a TV commercial, "Alpha-Bravo", which received an award as Best TV Commercial.

Between 1 and 3 October 1991 Stansted hosted the European Business Air Show, opened by Sir John Egan, the Chief Executive of BAA, and Eric Lomas. Twenty-eight aircraft ranging in

type from a Learjet to a Boeing 707 were assembled on the Business Terminal apron, and some transactions took place during the exhibition, which was regarded as being very successful.

FFV Aerotech, who had owned the maintenance hangar at Stansted since absorbing Qualitair Aviation in 1989, was itself bought by FLS Maintenance Ltd., a subsidiary of the huge Danish group FLS Industries A/S, in November 1991.

During the week before Christmas, over 33,000 passengers flew from or to Stansted on 815 flights, bringing the 1991 total to 1,700,000. The programme of winter scheduled services involved the continued expansion of Air UK and Ryanair flights, and although Ryanair dropped its Munich route it transferred its Cork service from Luton to Stansted. Air France was another operator who expressed a wish to use Stansted for more flights in the future, but a rationalisation plan caused a complete change of mind in January 1992, and the airline ceased flying from Stansted at the end of the winter season. Crossair, which had been flying from Stansted to Zurich, also departed when it moved its terminal to City Airport at the end of January, and Air Littoral ceased its services to Biarritz and Montpelier for the time being, pending clarification of licencing.

A third Russian aircraft was acquired by Heavylift in January 1992, this time an Il.76, CCCP-76758, which was put into service in Heavylift colours on oil pollution work. It was announced at that time that one of the An.124s

BAe 146-300QT of TNT, but operated by Air Foyle and in the colours of XP Parcel Express Systems, is seen on the cargo apron. [author]

Once inside the Passenger Terminal, the main concourse is light, bright and airy...

...with shops, banks, restaurants and snack-bars, car hire and every facility the traveller could require. [both Simon Peters]

was to be dedicated to a contract for European Airbus, flying between Toulouse, Manchester and Bremen, the second aircraft joining in after a year. By April 1992, a third An.124 had been added to the fleet, but in mid-1992 Heavylift Volga Dneiper was told by the CAA that the An.124s could not be operated in UK airspace until the new Russian authorities had provided appropriate certification. The three aircraft were therefore used elsewhere for a time, and Heavylift's Indonesian-registered Hercules aircraft were seen more frequently at Stansted.

The spring of 1992 brought news of further possible expansion to transatlantic traffic at Stansted when on 13 March United Airlines revealed that it planned to operate six flights from New York via Stansted, carrying spectators to the Olympic Games at Barcelona, but in the event these flights did not materialise. In addition, Northwest Airlines proposed to carry fly/cruise passengers on seventeen Boeing 747 flights from Minneapolis to Barcelona, returning from Venice and calling at Stansted in both directions. A third proposal was made by Rich International, which wanted to fly twice weekly in August and September 1992 from Orlando, Florida, to Stansted on behalf of Chieftain Tours.

Stansted's first scheduled service to Spain began on 1 April 1992, when Aviaco opened a route to Oviedo and Zaragoza, operated by DC-9s three times per week. Another destination was Havana, Cuba, to where Cubana began flying Il-62 aircraft on behalf of four tour operators every other week from 13 April.

Two million passengers!

Five months after the millionth passenger had passed through Stansted's new terminal, the two-millionth one followed, arriving on 22 April at 10.05 on a Ryanair BAC 1-11 from Dublin. At the end of May the twelve-month total was 2.1 million passengers, 60% of them using scheduled services, and the throughput continued to grow rapidly. The largest group of passengers handled so far, about 10,000 Italian and Spanish football supporters on their way to the European Cup Final, was dealt with successfully on 14 May. Much smaller in number was the party of veterans of the 344th Bomb Group, who visited Stansted on 2 May to see the changes made since they left the airfield in 1944 and to unveil a plaque in the terminal building to the memory of their colleagues.

During the twelve months to the end of May 1992, cargo handled at Stansted increased by 30% to nearly 42,000 tonnes, carried by more than twenty airlines. Most was flown by aircraft of Federal Express, Aeroflot, Southern Air Transport, Federal Express and UPS, which had embarked on a substantial expansion of flights using Stansted as a hub. A great increase in the quantity of freight being flown to or from the former Soviet Union had also begun.

American Airlines inaugurated its Chicago

Air UK's Fokker 100 G-UKFI is seen parked at a jetway on the International satellite just after a storm has passed over.
[Simon Peters]

service on 16 June 1992 as previously arranged, and it proved to be very popular. In the first three months, over 20,000 passengers were carried by the airline's Boeing 767 aircraft on the route, and it was found that the most popular onward destination was Minneapolis. By this time, Stansted had become the fastest-growing airport in the UK, with passenger figures up 46% over the previous year, over a quarter of a million passing through in May. Expansion of the scheduled services had proved to be particularly significant, with over 800 flights per week to or from over forty destinations. A comparison with past figures revealed that passengers handled in August 1992 equalled those handled in the whole of 1982! Very prominent by this time was Ryanair, which was carrying over half a million passengers per year to or from Stansted.

Air UK's next development was the entry into service of Fokker 100 aircraft, which began proving flights into Stansted in July 1992 before entering service early in August on the Paris, Nice, Frankfurt and Scottish routes. Ryanair, however, returned three leased ATR.42 aircraft as a consequence of closing the airline's routes to Waterford, Galway and Kerry, which had suffered in the recession. Instead, Ryanair planned to concentrate on its services to Dublin, Cork, Shannon and Knock, which were flown by the BAC 1-11 fleet.

At the end of September 1992, Royal Mail inaugurated the 'Skynet' operation, involving hubs at Stansted, East Midlands, Bristol and Liverpool. This venture began to bring several aircraft to Stansted each night, including BAe 748s of Euroair on flights to and from Belfast, another 748 of Janes Aviation on a Leeds—Liverpool—Stansted route, a Short SD3-60 of Gill Aviation from Newcastle and two Saab 340s of Business Air flying between Norwich, Stansted and Bristol, and an Electra of Channel Express to and from Edinburgh.

Most travellers arrive at the airport having already obtained their tickets, but every airline operating from Stansted maintains ticketing facilities for either direct purchase or collection...

Stansted airport now consists of four clearly-defined operating areas: the passenger terminal and it's associated satellites, handling the growing throughput of passengers on scheduled or chartered flights; the cargo area, able to deal with an ever-expanding work-load; the business aviation area, located in the old terminal building and hangars on the north side of the airport complex; and the maintenance area, where work on the largest aircraft is carried out. Supporting the operation of all these areas is Air Traffic Control, which is operated by National Air Traffic Services on behalf of the airport authorities.

Business Aviation.

In addition to handling an ever-increasing number of passengers on scheduled and charter flights, Stansted Airport caters for many private and corporate business aircraft. A proposal announced in October 1991 to create the first Avitat business aviation centre in Europe at Stansted quickly came to fruition, and part of the old terminal building, on the north side of the airfield, was completely refurbished by Esso Petroleum, to whom the brand name Avitat belongs. The new Centre was officially opened by Sir John Egan on 18 September 1992 after being topped out by Alan Haselhurst MP on 17 June 1992. The £3.1 million facility was managed by Hunting Business Aviation, which employed J & T Design & Build to construct a new hangar of 2400 sq. m. (25825 sq. ft.) area, with offices and apron space, as the first stage of a long-term development plan. There are eleven aircraft stands, capable of accommodating aircraft up to Boeing 747. Facilities available to the business aircraft user include 24-hour customs and immigration, conference rooms, catering, flight planning and weather forecasting, with of course hotel and taxi reservations. Engineering services

for visiting aircraft are provided at all hours by Hunting Business Aviation. Also prominent is Inflight's Executive Jet Centre, which provides a 24-hour maintenance and servicing facility capable of handling aircraft up to the size of a BAe. 125.

Passenger facilities

Mechanical and electrical engineering services in such a building are highly complex, and were designed by BAA based upon experience gained at other airports. The cost of these facilities represented a large proportion of the total, and included the provision of air conditioning, baggage handling, lighting and power and the automatic transit system. Heating and lighting, and also TV monitors and signing, are contained within the 'trees', each of which contains a spiral staircase from the undercroft to allow for maintenance without disruption of the public areas.

In the new building, Departure and Arrival areas are on the single concourse level, where arriving and departing international passengers are segregated. Facilities on the concourse level are located within free-standing enclosures 5m. (16'4") high, and include shops, lounges, offices, 24-hour banks, catering, toilets, car rental companies, information desks and an inter-denominational chapel, and there are reservation desks for hotels and taxis.

Electrical and mechanical equipment is restricted to the 8.3m. (27ft.) high undercroft below. Detailed energy studies were carried out to analyse the heating and cooling requirements of the building, and it was found that by extracting waste heat from the busy commercial areas it would be possible to minimise the heat input during most of the winter months unless extreme weather is experienced. The resulting systems allow a much lower running cost than

...before moving on to the Check-In Desks.

*With the advent of electronic technology, gone are the days of a Desk for a specific flight. This line of Air UK desks are available for all destinations, the agents processing each client onto their flight via a computer terminal.
[both Simon Peters]*

THE STANSTED EXPERIENCE

It has been written somewhere that passing through an modern airport is the most complex journey a person could make.

Assisting the passengers 'on their way' by making sure that everything runs as smoothly as possible from behind the scenes is each airlines Passenger Services office - in this case Air UK's, staffed by Nicky Garrett and Gale Sparks.
[Simon Peters]

any earlier terminal buildings. Passing through the undercroft is a service road giving access to storage areas used by the concourse shops and to the staff restaurant.

Two 'satellites', of which the first, for international flights, was opened with the terminal building, form an integral part of the new terminal. The International satellite is connected to it by the 'People Mover' system below ground level, and can handle up to 1500 passengers per hour. It has nine Jetways (flexible connections to the boarding point of the aircraft) and seating for 1200 on a 7600sq.m. (81780sq.ft.) upper floor, with 13 escalators and three lifts to carry passengers between floor levels. The second satellite was opened in November 1993 and is currently in use for domestic flights. At present it is connected to the terminal building by a walkway, but will be extended as traffic grows. Stansted's Jetways range in length between 24m.

(78'9") and 55m. (180'6") and the three installed most recently are capable of fully automatic operation.

Stansted's 'People Mover' system of driverless trains was designed to allow for expansion to serve an eventual four satellites, and cost £30 million. At present, five cars, each with a capacity of 80 passengers, are in use, and can be coupled together if necessary into pairs or threes depending on the number of passengers needing to be moved. The maximum speed of the cars is 28 mph (45 kph), and they run on pneumatic rubber-tyred wheels on a concrete track, not a conventional rail system, guidance being by means of wheels on a central guide beam. Computers in the cars are linked with a co-ordinating computer in a central control room. At the International satellite, the trains switch onto the return track before picking up incoming passengers on their way to the terminal building.

A panoramic view of the Passenger Terminal area at Stansted...

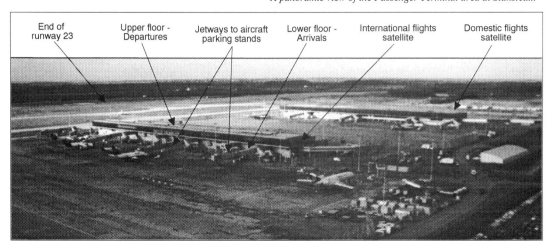

| End of runway 23 | Upper floor - Departures | Jetways to aircraft parking stands | Lower floor - Arrivals | International flights satellite | Domestic flights satellite |

TODAY AND TOMORROW

Movement from the Passenger Terminal to the Domestic satellite is via a walkway. Transit to the International satellite is by driverless, computer-controlled 'People Movers', which run for part of the journey underground. [Simon Peters]

Public transport to and from the airport received much attention during the planning stage, and apart from the road connection to the M11 motorway a railway branching off the main London (Liverpool Street) to Cambridge line was included in the project. Working closely with British Rail, BAA incorporated a railway station in the terminal design, resulting in easy access for passengers disembarking from trains. Escalators, lifts and ramps minimise walking distances. The single-track line leaves the terminal building in a tunnel which carries it under the runway and motorway, and the track then doubles before splitting to allow for both southbound and northbound departures and arrivals.

Passengers arriving at Stansted airport by road use the long-stay car park, which can accommodate 8000 cars and is connected to the terminal building about four miles (6.5km.) away by a frequent free bus service. 'Meeters' and others not planning to remain at the terminal for long may use the 2300-space short-term car park nearby.

Interesting statistics released towards the end of 1992 indicated that nearly 40% of Stansted's passengers were people in socio-economic groups A and B, while 38% were in group C1. Almost 62% of the passengers were using cars to travel to the airport, and only 18% used the trains. In terms of the catchment area, 70% of passengers originated in London or south-east England and 21% in East Anglia. Flights taken by 80% of passengers were for leisure purposes. Residents of the UK made up 66% of the passengers, with a further 20% from the EEC countries.

An Airbus A.300 aircraft of European Airlines brought 171 refugees of the Bosnian conflict from Skopje in the former Yugoslavia on 10 November 1992, and to house them temporarily the old terminal building was pressed into service. Contingency plans were then discussed by the Stansted Airport management and the Uttlesford District Council in preparation of the arrival of further refugee flights.

By the autumn, schedules for the winter of 1992/93 were being arranged, and several new routes were planned. Among them were thrice-weekly services to Barcelona and Madrid by Aviaco DC-9; Copenhagen and Gröningen twice a day by Jetstream aircraft of BASE; and Manchester three times a day and Waterford daily

...that gives some idea as to the scale and logic to the layout. [both Simon Peters].

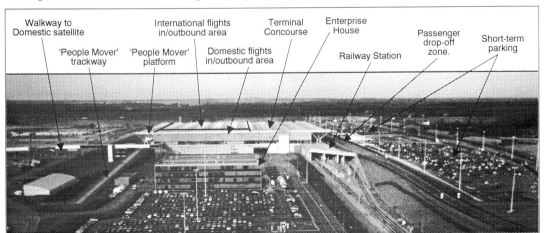

| Walkway to Domestic satellite | International flights in/outbound area | Terminal Concourse | Enterprise House | Passenger drop-off zone. | Short-term parking |

'People Mover' trackway   'People Mover' platform   Domestic flights in/outbound area   Railway Station

If travelling abroad, after passing through Passport Control the passenger arrives in the International Tax and Duty Free Concourse, where a number of shops offer a full range of goods. There are also more-than-ample rest areas, with views overlooking the Domestic satellite. [Simon Peters]

by Manx Airlines Jetstream. The Waterford route potentially added to the large number of passengers being carried to Irish airports from Stansted - now the second main departure airport in the UK for Irish traffic. Passenger figures for 1992 revealed that 2,330,000 had been handled at Stansted, an increase of 39% over 1991, and of these 69% were on scheduled flights.

Stansted's brief period as an RAF Station at the end of the Second World War was remembered when in February 1993 an Air Training Corps. unit, 1096 (Stansted Airport) Detached Flight, was established in the old police station premises on First Avenue.

Further development of the cargo business took place on 1 March 1993, when Federal Express switched its operation from Heathrow to Stansted. Offering a 'next-day-by-10.30' delivery service across the USA, FedEx used DC-10s between Stansted and New York and Memphis, Boeing 727s from Paris to Stansted, and Friendships from Cologne, Frankfurt, Milan and Basle.

Another milestone was reached on 28 March 1993, when Aeroflot inaugurated a twice-weekly service from St. Petersburg, the first to Stansted from a Russian destination, following the success

of three charter flights. On the first flight, rows of seats were removed from the aircraft to allow space for stacks of shoes, clothing and electrical goods being taken home by Russian businessmen for sale to a starved market! The charter was arranged by Maverique, a small trading company and a similar organisation in Moscow, and the Russians who travelled spent over £350,000 in London during their trip.

Discussions on the plans for a diversion of the A120 main road continued with a public enquiry early in June. Subsequently, a memorandum of understanding was signed concerning part of the new road to be built within the airport boundary. Close to the terminal, the Domestic satellite was under construction during the summer of 1993,

Not only are adult travellers cared for in the Departure Lounges at Stansted. To keep the younger passengers interested - like Ryan and Shannon Heffernan waiting for their flight to the Republic of Ireland - Airtours have sponsored the Children's Club playzone. [Simon Peters]

for partial completion in November. On the airport's north side, a new 3600 sq. m. (38736 sq. ft.) hangar was opened on 7 July 1993 for Inflite to use as its Executive Jet Centre. This company, which operates round the clock, employed 150 people to give full maintenance support to the owners of business jet aircraft.

Early April brought the bad news that American Airlines would cease flying its Chicago service, and on 31 May the last flight took off, after over 60,000 passengers had been carried on the route in its ten months of operation. Unfortunately, this figure represented a low yield factor, and £6.6 million had been lost by American Airlines on the route. Meanwhile, on 19 April, TWA had confirmed that it intended to operate a replacement service, calling additionally at New York, and provided US Government approval was obtained would open the service on 1 June. This plan came to nothing, and on 10 June John McGregor (the Secretary of State for Transport) stated that he would only allow a US carrier to operate a new route to Stansted provided Virgin Atlantic was permitted to serve Boston from Heathrow. A temporary licence for TWA's proposed service was ruled out. Three weeks later, Mr. McGregor finally turned down TWA's application, despite representation from Stansted Airport, Alan Haselhurst MP, the CBI, Uttlesford District Council, Essex County Council, the Guild of

Business Travel Agents and many other interested parties. In a last-ditch attempt to persuade Mr. McGregor to change his mind, a delegation of trade unionists gathered at the airport on 22 July, but to no avail. Had TWA's service been allowed, the 400,000 people who it was believed wished to travel to the United States from the Stansted catchment area each year would have been saved the frustrating journey round the M25 motorway to Heathrow.

July 1993 passenger numbers showed yet another significant increase and a twelve-month total of nearly 2.5 million. Scheduled services and IT charter flights had both increased, and for the month of August Ryanair added an extra 348 flights to its already intensive programme. In October new services to Kortrijk in Belgium by Sky Service and to Izmir by Turkish Airlines became operative and the most extensive winter IT programme ever mounted from Stansted was announced. The major destinations covered were Tenerife and Lanzarote in the Canary Islands. At the same time, restrictions on night-time flights were imposed. Calculated on a points system, the number of movements at night between 24 October 1993 and 27 March 1994 was set at 5000. Hard on the heels of the winter programme came the plans for the summer of 1994, which showed a 12% increase in available seats! It was stated that Stansted passengers were younger than those using the other two London airports and

Above: the dedicated cargo area, used for freight shipping concerns and air package companies.
[Simon Peters]
As much of this work is conducted at night-time, it is not surprising that many operators make use of the 'good neighbour whisperjet' the BAe 146.
Right: a pair of 146QTs (Quiet Traders) of TNT Express Worldwide rest during the hours of daylight.
[author]

were more likely to be making their first flights. They had a tendency to buy whisky rather than other spirits from the duty-free shops.

Chief Executive of BAA Sir John Egan came to Stansted on 1 November 1993 to open the new Domestic satellite. Built at a cost of £3 million and completed ahead of schedule, the new 'finger' gives access on one level direct from the terminal building 200 metres (219 yards) away.

By the end of 1993, freight throughput at Stansted had reached 60,000 tonnes per year, almost two-thirds of which was carried on scheduled cargo flights by Federal Express, Aeroflot and Turkish Airlines. Among the unusual items carried had been a three-tonne killer whale to Florida and 350 pigs to Cuba.

Next to come into use was a 3500sq.m. (37,660sq.ft.) bonded warehouse for TNT Express Worldwide, which was opened on 1 January 1994, and future developments include another 4000 sq.m. (43,040 sq.ft.) of warehousing, a new freight agents' building and 26 acres of land for warehousing and industry.

Increased income from landing fees and the retail operation, with tight cost control, enabled a forecast of a financial break-even in 1997. By then, the passenger throughput figures for 1993 had become available, showing that scheduled flights carried 23.9% more than in 1992 and IT charters 27.1% more. The 1993 total, 2.67 million passengers, indicated that total growth had been 14.5%. Travellers to and from Eire, in particular, had grown at the rate of 34%. Measures to cope with the expected continuation of the upward trend would have to be considered!

New routes announced for the 1994 summer season included three by Air UK — to Copenhagen, Belfast (City) and Munich. Air Engiadina would fly to Berne, Teesside Aviation to Teesside, Turkish Airlines to Antalya, and Air Littoral would re-open its Biarritz service. New charters would bring the return of Scandinavian business, and British World planned to operate flights for the Ministry of Defence.

Caring for the environment

Even before development work on the new terminal complex began, Essex County Council archeologists excavated a Late Iron Age village and a Roman burial ground and farm on the site. In doing so they found several brooches, coins, pieces of pottery and other artefacts, many of which are on display in Saffron Walden museum. From the Iron Age village, located where the Cargo Centre now stands, Italian wine flagons were recovered, revealing that the site was a centre of international trade 2000 years ago! Seven 'listed' cottages, barns and stables were carefully dismantled and re-erected elsewhere.

In planning the new Stansted airport, considerable funds were allocated to providing an attractive environment which at the same time would allow the continuation, and indeed development, of wildlife habitats. A quarter of a million trees and shrubs of indigenous species were planted at a cost of £3 miilion and over 30,000 plants were used to create 4.5 km. (2.8 miles) of hedgerows. Roughly 10% of the total airport area — 86 hectares (213 acres) — has been landscaped and 6.5 million cu.m. (8.4

BAe 146-200QC G-ZAPK of Titan Airways is loaded with another cargo of palletised freight. [Simon Peters]

miilion cu.yds.) of soil were moved within the site, a planning stipulation being that no soil could be removed from the airport. An area of 4 hectares (10 acres) was set aside so that eight parcels of ancient grassland which fostered 78 plant species, including such rarities as the bee orchid, could be conserved after being moved from elsewhere in the airport complex. Over 60 hectares (148 acres) were allocated for new woodlands and copses, care being taken to ensure compatability with exisiting woodland. Roadside banked areas and other locations amounting to 30 hectares (74 acres) were sown with seeds of wild flowers. There is even a Site of Special Scientific Interest, East End Wood, which is managed by the airport authority. The task of maintaining the airfield's grassed and wooded areas is in the hands of the Landscape Engineer Tony Ogden, whose staff cut the grass six times each year, resulting in the removal of about 550 tonnes of grass and weeds. Tony says that his ambition is

"to train the airport rabbits to munch their way through grass in neat lines at the right height"!

The reduction of aircraft noise is treated very seriously, and to minimise the effect of aircraft taking off on runway 23 (to the south-west) an eleven-metre (36 ft.) high soil bank was formed to shield the residents of the hamlet of Molehill Green, on the north-east side of the airport. A 24-hour NTK (Noise & Track Keeping) system operating up to ten miles (16 km.) from the airport to an altitude of 10,000 feet (about 3000m.) monitors adherence to the noise limits and to preferential routes for take-off. Monitoring equipment is located at positions determined by the Dept. of Transport, and mobile units can be set up wherever needed. All the information recorded during a 24-hour period is collated by computer at midnight each night, allowing a map to be printed out showing the exact track of every aircraft and the noise level it created. Take-offs and landings between 23.30 and 06.30 are

During an aircraft turn-around an airliner is surrounded by specialist vehicles and items of equipment, some of which are easily identified, others whose uses are not quite so obvious.

Left: As the pilot brings the aircraft up to its parking spot, the jetway - that covered walkway used by passengers to embark and disembark - is driven into position The jetway can be swung in an arc, extended, raised or lowered to match the height and position of the aircraft's main cabin door. A canopy can then be extended to protect the passengers from the elements when boarding. The aircraft interior is cleaned and restocked after every flight -and that includes re-filling the aircraft's fresh water supply (upper right). Bottom right: Baggage can be containerized in the terminal and loaded into the holds of larger aircraft. On smaller aircraft, such as Air UK's Fokker 100 Uniform Delta, baggage handlers bring the items out to the aircraft on covered trolleys and load the cases aboard by hand. [all Simon Peters]

THE STANSTED EXPERIENCE

This pair of pictures show Air UK 146-300 G-UKSC during turn-around before departing on UKA978 to Dusseldorf. The nose of the aircraft can be seen alongside the jetway, with the Servisair aircraft tug connected to the nosewheel in front and the scissor-lift catering truck alongside...

.. whilst .under one wing, away from the jetway is a Stansted Fuelling Co. fuel truck, pumping kerosene into the aircraft from the underground fuel supply piped to each aircraft parking stand. Another supply truck, this time from Alpha Flight Services is at the rear door of the 146.
[both Simon Peters]

limited, the noise levels of different types of aircraft being taken into account, with a view to encouraging the use of quieter aircraft. Airlines breaching the take-off noise limits are fined and the money received is distributed to worthy local organisations.

Guided tours of the airport have been available to the public for many years, and members of many different types of organisation take advantage of this opportunity. A special check-in desk in the terminal building is the starting point for groups of not less than ten people. Lasting about two hours, tours are escorted by an experienced guide who provides a commentary on Stansted's history, development and current services. For this facility, a small charge is levied to cover administrative costs.

Aircraft handling and passenger services
Two companies are responsible for ensuring that passengers and freight and the aircraft on which they are travelling are handled efficiently at Stansted — Servisair plc, which has about 92% of the 'ramp' business, and Gatwick Handling International Ltd. After originating at Manchester airport, Servisair set up a branch at Stansted in April 1968, with a staff of three. From that small beginning the Stansted operation has grown to employ 435 staff, who are responsible for ground handling of aircraft on the aprons, the passenger ticketing and boarding system for most airlines, and baggage and cargo handling. At Stansted this currently involves, on average, over a hundred departures each 24-hour period. A typical day, 19 September 1996, involved the handling of 239

Pushback! Cleaned, refuelled, re-supplied and with new passengers and baggage, Air UK Flight UKA768 is pushed away from the International satellite by a Servicair aircraft tug to begin its short flight to Amsterdam. [Simon Peters]

movements, including ten mail flights, nine cargo flights and nine positioning flights. Seventeen basic types of aircraft belonging to twenty-two airlines, flying to or from 56 airports, were dealt with that day. To co-ordinate the task, two members of staff man an operations room. International discreet telex terminals (SITA) are used for early notification of the time of an aircraft's arrival at Stansted, while a dedicated VHF radio channel allows the crew of an inbound aircraft to notify Servisair of its requirements of fuel and other supplies and to confirm its time of arrival. Requests for medical assistance or the use of a wheelchair are also dealt with in this way. This information is fed selectively into a common computer system by means of which arrival times are entered on the large displays in the terminal building, fuel and in-flight catering supplies are arranged and aircraft cleaners are advised of their imminent task. Servisair is now the largest independent handling agent in Europe, operating at 61 airports in six European Union coutries, and has 300 airline customers, but passengers passing through the airport are unlikely to be aware of the considerable effort which goes into making their journeys trouble-free.

In response to the ever-growing demands made by the airlines, a £600,000 project to increase the passenger-handling capacity began on 6 April 1994. Three more telescopic bridges were provided at the International satellite, with extra gates so that one stand could handle two aircraft at the same time. This improvement was followed on 10 June by the announcement of a project valued at £2.2 million for the expansion of facilities for domestic passengers. New apron areas were constructed, and the size of the passenger lounge doubled, with completion set for the end of July.

Plans for the first direct flights from Stansted to the west coast of the United States were announced in April 1994 by Leisure Air, which operated charters twice each week to San Francisco between 30 May and 24 September 1994, using DC-10 aircraft. Closer to home, the route to Metz/Nancy which Luxair had flown until March 1993 was taken over on 7 June by Proteus, which employed Beech 200 aircraft on the daily service. Other new services for summer operation included an Air UK route to Milan and two by new airline Euro Direct, to Hamburg and Humberside, both starting at the end of August.

The main event of the summer of 1994 was, however, when the Government announced on 15 July that approval of a transatlantic service from Stansted outside the existing bilateral agreement would be granted. US airlines would be invited to apply for a daily service to Chicago via New York, in which TWA and Tower Air had already expressed interest. This fundamental act was restated on 12 October by Dr. Brian Mawhinney, who had in the meantime taken over from John McGregor as Secretary of State for Transport. He confirmed that unrestricted transatlantic scheduled services would be approved, and urged the US Government to respond in a like manner.

Continued increases in cargo business at Stansted prompted plans to be made in August 1994 to increase the original 9000 sq.m. bonded warehouse by 3500 sq.m. Stansted was now the fourth largest air-freight depot in the UK, handling by July 1994 76,620 tonnes per year. Another cargo service was introduced on 19 August to boost the figures still further, when Air China began a weekly flight from Peking using Boeing 747s.

Stansted's three-millionth passenger in a year left on a flight to Edinburgh on 25 August 1994 and the upward trend in both passenger and cargo use continued, the latter reaching a figure of almost 80,000 tonnes per annum in September. Five days a week from 31 October, a BAC 1-11 leased from European Aviation Air Charter was flown by new airline ALEX (Aberdeen London Express), which had been founded by former

British World Airlines'series 531 BAC 1-11 G-OBWE. [Simon Peters]

Bishops Stortford resident Dr. Robert Perryment. A unique scheduled service to Havana by Cubana took the place of their fortnightly charter flights from 24 October, when Il.62s began flying the route every Thursday.

Further improvement work at Stansted came to fruition in December 1994, when a new lounge dedicated to Belfast traffic was opened. Situated next to the main domestic lounge in No.2 satellite, the new facility had cost £200,000, and was in good time to be used by passengers on a new service five times each day to Belfast International Airport opened by Air Belfast on 1 March 1995.

Air Traffic Control.
Construction of the long-needed new control tower to replace the enlarged and altered wartime-vintage building on the north side of the runway began in December, and a foundation stone was laid in February by Derek McLauchlan, chief executive of National Air Traffic Services. By the end of March 1995 progress in the ground by the contractors, Trafalgar House, allowed the rapid concreting of the 60-metre (197ft.) high cylindrical structure to begin. Pouring concrete by night and day, Trafalgar House completed this stage of the £5 million contract in four weeks! During July the mechanical services room and the visual control room which tops the building were under construction, while at ground level the administrative section of the tower was almost complete. The new tower came into use at the end of February 1996, and was formally opened by BAA Chief Executive Sir John Egan on 17 May.

Located close to the cargo area on land leased from the airport by National Air Traffic Services, is the new control tower. The new building contains the latest equipment for use by the air traffic control staff, who from the visual control room at the top of the slender structure have a clear view of all passenger and cargo areas as well as the whole length of the runway and taxi-tracks. In fair weather, it is easy to see aircraft ten miles away, beyond Thaxted, lining up to land on runway 23, while in the opposite direction Canary Wharf can be seen.

At the foot of the tower is a two-storey block containing, on the ground floor, the engineering department. Here, mounted on racks, is the computer, VHF radio and ground radar equipment. with full test facilities. On a series of consoles are mounted repeaters of the displays seen in the control room and of the area radar

display. The first floor contains the administrative and management staff. A high-speed lift takes staff to floor 13, the projecting part of the tower, where staff rest rooms are located. From here a staircase climbs to the control room some 197 feet (60m.) above ground level.

On duty at any one time are two controllers, one handling air movements and one ground movements, with help from two assistants. Whereas previously Stansted boasted its own radar room on the ground floor of the old tower complex, radar approaches to Stansted are now handled by a dedicated controller working at the London Air Traffic Control Centre at West Drayton (LATCC). For example, an aircraft approaching over the Essex coast from Amsterdam is firstly handled by an Area controller, who then passes the movement to Terminal North controller, who guides the aircraft down to lower altitudes. He or she in turn passes the aircraft to the Stansted Approach controller. whose task, using a radar display, is to position the aircraft onto the Stansted instrument

The new Control Tower under construction, seen the day after the services ring was hoisted up into position on 4 July 1995. On top of this ring was constructed the Visual Control Room [Author]

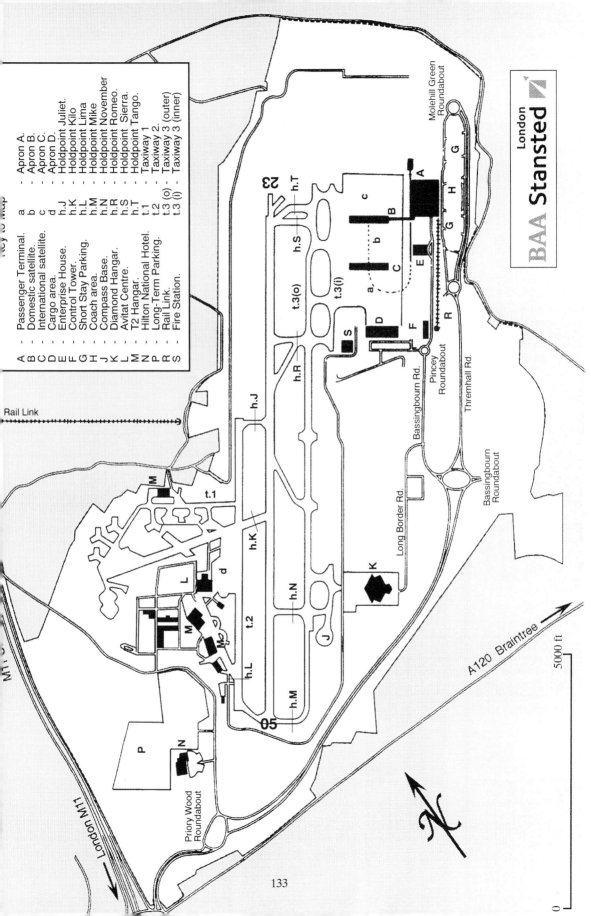

Key to Map

A	–	Passenger Terminal.	a – Apron A.
B	–	Domestic satellite.	b – Apron B.
C	–	International satellite.	c – Apron C.
D	–	Cargo area.	d – Apron D.
E	–	Enterprise House.	h.J – Holdpoint Juliet.
F	–	Control Tower.	h.K – Holdpoint Kilo.
G	–	Short Stay Parking.	h.L – Holdpoint Lima.
H	–	Coach area.	h.M – Holdpoint Mike.
J	–	Compass Base.	h.N – Holdpoint November.
K	–	Diamond Hangar.	h.R – Holdpoint Romeo.
L	–	Avitat Centre.	h.S – Holdpoint Sierra.
M	–	T2 Hangar.	h.T – Holdpoint Tango.
N	–	Hilton National Hotel.	t.1 – Taxiway 1.
P	–	Long-Term Parking.	t.2 – Taxiway 2.
R	–	Rail Link.	t.3 (o) – Taxiway 3 (outer)
S	–	Fire Station.	t.3 (i) – Taxiway 3 (inner)

London
BAA Stansted

Rail Link

London M11

M11

A120 Braintree

Long Border Rd.

Bassingbourn Rd.

Thremhall Rd.

Molehill Green Roundabout

Pincey Roundabout

Bassingbourn Roundabout

Priory Wood Roundabout

5000 ft

23

05

133

landing system (ILS) or to ensure that the pilot is in visual contact. These three controllers are all at LATCC and thus never see the aircraft they are handling. Finally, the aircraft is handed over to the air controller in Stansted tower, who ensures that there is no conflicting air traffic and oversees the landing.

To handle movements on the ground, the appropriate controller uses a display known as Surface Movement Radar (SMR), which shows the locality of every aircraft and vehicle within the manoeuvring area. The controller is responsible for approving the initial start-up and push-back of departing aircraft and for directing pilots to the runway in use and also for guiding each incoming aircraft to its parking bay.

Apart from handling telephone calls, the two control assistants look after the documentation of all aircraft movements, of which the average number is 300 per day at present, peaking at 330. Nowadays, flight plans are dealt with by means of the Integrated Flight Planning System (IFPS), which is centralised at Brussels. Flight plans are communicated on the Aeronautical Fixed Telecommunications Network (AFTN). It is also the duty of one of the assistants to make a status report every twenty minutes on Aerodrome Terminal Information Service (ATIS), which is effectively a broadcast recorded on a loop system then transmitted for reception by pilots and other concerned parties and has superseded Volmet broadcasts. Contained in ATIS is information on the weather, runway condition and any other pertinent factors.

More services
British Airways Express scheduled flights came to Stansted for the first time in January 1995, when Manx Airlines converted its Waterford, Shannon and Manchester routes to a franchise operation flown by aircraft in BA colours. Northern Ireland was again featured on 27 March 1995, when new airline Macair began flying a twice-daily schedule to Londonderry using 19-seat Jetstream 31 aircraft. Scandinavian charter flights had come back with a vengeance by this time, showing passenger figures which had increased by 50% in a year. Air UK was Stansted's most active airline, and in March 1995 added the former Euro Direct's service to Hamburg to its route system. Ryanair came second in passenger and flight terms, with Britannia Airways' charter flights third, all helping to boost Stansted passenger figures to 3.3 million in the twelve months ending 20 February 1995. The main users of Stansted's cargo facilities were Federal Express, TNT and THY Turkish Airlines. Stansted's general aviation terminal also recorded an increase in traffic over the twelve months to the end of March 1995. During that period, 105,000 passengers on corporate or private flights had used the facility, 12% more than the previous year, many of whom found the conference rooms a great advantage.

The Visual Control Room at the very top of the Control Tower offers supurb panoramic views of the Airport and Essex countryside. [Simon Peters]

Measures to discourage the use of noisy aircraft at Stansted were strengthened in April 1995, when landing charges became even more weighted against offending airlines. From that date, the noisiest aircraft were charged up to 55% more than the quietest, a very significant deterrent and proof that the authorities were working to minimise the environmental impact of the airport.

As an aid to local companies as well as to the airport's own fire service, a purpose-built training centre was opened on 8 June 1995 in the former fire station. The sum of £65,000 was spent on refurbishment and fitting out, and courses on all aspects of this vital service began, under the management of Station Officer Peter Harding.

In May 1995, passengers using domestic flights from or to Stansted increased in number by no less than 77% compared with the same month in 1994, a total of 57,000 passengers making use of services to Aberdeen, the two Belfast airports, Edinburgh, Glasgow, Derry, Manchester and Newcastle. In part, the huge increase was due to the advent of Air Belfast and Jersey European, but Air UK added to the total by increasing fights on its Aberdeen and Edinburgh routes. The total passenger throughput in May was 333,000, an increase of 12% over May 1994, bringing the annual figure to 3.4 million. Adding to the thirteen existing destinations in Spain were Bilbao and Barcelona, two cities served from 25 June by charter flights organised by tour operator Frantour/Travelnow. Cubana's weekly service to Havana was extended on 15 June 1995 to Kingston and Montego Bay in Jamaica, a service unique to Stansted.

The only aircraft able to carry such an awkward load, the Antonov An.124, took off on 8 June carrying four ships fenders 12'1" (3.7m.) in

diameter by 22'0" (6.7m.) long to West Africa. Arranged by Heavylift at short notice on behalf of Norfolk-based Fender Care Ltd., the flight enabled the transfer of crude oil off Abidjan to proceed with minimal delay.

Passenger figures continued to grow, with 430,455 travellers using Stansted in July 1995, an increase of 17% over the previous July. No passengers were carried, however, on the DC-10 of Orbis International, which arrived in August 1995. This aircraft is a flying eye hospital, complete with an operating theatre, and was parked free of charge at Stansted for three weeks before flying to Bulgaria on one of Orbis' missions.

Further expansion

On 28 August 1995 it was announced that plans for the investment of a further £100 million in Stansted airport were being drawn up, to include the construction of two further satellites. Proposals to increase the maximum number of Air Transport Movements at Stansted from 78,000 to 150,000 per annum were put before Parliament, as it had been found that the use of smaller than expected aircraft by the main airlines had resulted in fewer passengers per movement

Whether the traveller is going aboard (right) or within the United Kingdom (below), the Departure Gates at Stansted all have spacious seating areas with full passenger facilities close to hand. [Simon Peters]

Also going across the Irish Sea is BAe 146 EI-CLU of Aer Lingus Commuter. [Simon Peters]

than estimated, with the result that the earlier limit, set in 1987, had been almost reached. The proposal would allow 15 million passengers per year to use the airport, for which planning permission already exisited, and would create a further 5000 jobs over the next five years.

The winter 1995/96 schedules of flights from Stansted included a new three-times-per-week service to Newark, New Jersey, by the Israeli flag-carrier El Al, which was able to operate outside the UK/US bilateral air service agreement as it had 'fifth freedom rights' to carry passengers between London and New York. On these flights, Superstar Holidays offered a return fare of £167 plus airport taxes. El Al also offered flights to its home base at Tel Aviv, while Aviaco added a route to La Corruna, Air UK established itself on the Paris (Charles de Gaulle) route and Ryanair opened a service to Prestwick for Glasgow. A new IT service involved BAC 1-11 and BAe.146 aircraft of British World Airlines, which between December 1995 and April 1996 flew to Lourdes, carrying not pilgrims but skiers on behalf of TT Ski.

Operation *'Christmas Child'* took place on 16 December 1995, when an Antonov aircraft of Heavylift took off for Zagreb laden with 80,000 shoe boxes containing gifts for children in Bosnia,Croatia and Serbia. Four similar flights followed, destinations being Rumania, Slovakia, Hungary and Moscow, with a final trip to Rwanda. Staff at the airport and local school children embraced the charity with enthusiasm, and collected enough gifts to fill 4000 of the boxes. On the Rwanda flight was a shoe-box handed over by three-year-old Anthony Morgan, son of Stansted Airport's Managing Director, Terry Morgan.

Stansted's best year ever ended on 31 March 1996, when it was announced that in the previous twelve months 4,129,071 passengers had used the airport, an increase of 23%. Freight handled totalled 94,000 tonnes, a figure third only to Heathrow and Gatwick. At the same time an interesting set of statistics about Stansted airport was published, revealing that Stansted had become the sixth largest airport in the United Kingdom. For the previous five years Stansted had enjoyed a 20% average growth — the fastest growth of any major UK airport. Three quarters of its passengers flew on scheduled services (more than from Gatwick or Manchester), the most popular route being to Dublin. 23% of passengers used the Skytrain train service to London. Broken down into socio-economic groups, passengers of group AB constitued 42% of the total, C1 39%, C2 12% and D/E 7%. Greater London provided 35% of the passengers, the south-east 36% and East Anglia 21%, and the balance came from further afield. In gender terms, 64% of passengers were male and 36% female, while 48% were between 25 and 44 years of age. At the same time, a survey conducted by the French *'Aeroports'* magazine placed Stansted at 38th in the league of airports in the fifteen EU countries.

Eleven new routes from Stansted for the 1996 season included four scheduled flights per week to Prague by CSA Czech Airlines' Boeing 737; to Rotterdam 17 times per week by Air UK's BAe 146s; daily flights to Dublin by Aer Lingus; and a daily service to Marseilles by Jersey European and Air Inter. New charter services were to Venice with British World Airlines on behalf of Cosmos; Calvi (Corsica) by Air UK for Holiday Options; Minneapolis by Rich International; and to Toronto with Air Club International. Charter flights from Geneva and Zurich on behalf of Swiss IT operator Falcon Travel, with outward tours operated by Plus Travel, began on 1 April, using BAe.146 and ATP aircraft of Flightline. Of great significance was IT operator Unijet's service to Orlando, Florida, which opened on 19 May, flown by Leisure International Boeing 767-300ER aircraft. Using this route, Unijet offered fourteen-night holidays at Kissimmee from £439, which included a rental car and accommodation, or a similar holiday at Disney World for £589.

Although the new passenger terminal had been opened almost five years earlier, a certain amount of unrest among local residents persisted. In the BBC television programme 'Matter Of Fact', broadcast in February 1996, Mr. Norman Mead, General Secretary of the Preservation Association and member of the Airport Consultative Committee, said of the airport

"...It is like Dante's inferno when it is running at its peak, and is something to which no civilised society should be subjected. Essex is very often written off as a no-man's land by many, although north-west Essex is rich in many things — rolling countryside, high-grade agricultural land, listed buildings, conservation areas, areas of special landscape value, listed hedgerows and protected lanes. We have them all here, with ancient towns such as Thaxted and Saffron Walden. There is just so much at stake which is part of our English heritage and we are damned if we are going to let that be affected by commercial interests. The underlying feeling now is that we need jobs but also we need our heritage and the space that we know". Mr. Mead went on to say "...when people look out of their windows and see across the airport the second largest aircraft in the world coming at them at low level, its engines at full bore, fear is very much in their minds".

Alterations to the approach patterns used by aircraft inbound to Stansted came into effect in April 1996. Between 23.00 and 07.00, aircraft must not descend below an altitude of 3000 feet (915m.), rather than the previous level of 2000 feet (610m.), until becoming established on final approach. Smaller propeller-driven aircraft must be established by four miles from touch-down and must not descend below 2000 feet until on final approach. Improvements to the noise and track monitoring equipment were made at a cost of £50,000, allowing a more rapid response to be made to any complaints. In a Gallop poll taken among residents in the Uttlesford District Council area, about a third said that aircraft noise was a disadvantage to living near the airport, but 75% considered that Stansted airport was a benefit to the community.

France's principal IT operator, Nouvelles Frontières, announced in May that between 13 June and 22 September 1996 it would operate twice-weekly flights to Rome and Milan, using Boeing 737-200 aircraft owned by Air Charter International. About a quarter of the passengers were expected to originate in England.

Sunday 2 June 1996 brought a wide range of aircraft to Stansted, from where they took part in a fly-past over London to mark the 50th anniversary of the opening of London Heathrow airport. Among the aircraft seen at Stansted that day were two examples of the DH.89 Dragon Rapide, as used at Heathrow in the nineteen-fifties for pleasure flights; the sole remaining

Dublin-based Ryanair standardised their fleet around the Boeing 737 series of airliners, EI-CJF is seen here about to depart for Knock. [Simon Peters]

airworthy DH.104 Comet, which pioneered jet transport; the Bristol Freighter, coincidentally a Stansted regular for many years; Concorde; and several contemporary airliners. After the fly-past, several of the participants overflew the Imperial War Museum at Duxford during an air show before returning to Stansted.

Housing for Stansted employees again came to the forefront in July 1996, when the parish councils of Felsted, Takeley, Birchanger and Little Dunmow, acting with a local conservation group, lost a High Court fight to save their *"quintessentially English"* way of life. A ten-year plan drawn up by Uttlesford District Council in 1990 to reflect Stansted's expansion had forecast a growth in the number of workers needing housing from 3500 to 14,500. The Council had favoured a single-site development on the former Great Dunmow airfield, but in 1993 a public enquiry decided on dispersal of 2500 new homes throughout the four parishes, 650 in Felsted, 625 in Great Dunmow, 400 in Stansted Mountfitchet (mostly in Birchanger parish), and 825 in Takeley. In a statement, a representative of the four parishes said that they were *"saddened "* by the decision, which would mean that the characters of the villages would be devastated, and the Chairman of the Felsted & Little Dunmow Conservative Association said that the plan would *"...effectively mean doom"* for the chosen areas.

Britain's twelve top show-jumping and dressage team horses in the 1996 Olympic Games were flown to Atlanta, Georgia from Stansted, where they were handled by Servisair, along with other horses which were loaded on board five specially-adapted Boeing 747 cargo aircraft of Lufthansa.

Record figures were again achieved during June—August 1996, when passenger numbers rose by a further 27% compared with the similar period of 1995. The annual passenger throughput was now running at 4.4 million. Routes flown from Stansted totalled 43, with new summer services to Marseilles, Prague, Rotterdam, Santander and Santiago, Spain. July saw the half-million per month figure exceeded for the first time, a 16.9% increase over the previous July. Although nationally a fall in the short-haul charter business was felt, figures for this business at Stansted rose by 5%.

Stansted was in the news again on 5 August 1996, when a party of 112 Russian children and eight adults who had been attending a month-long language course in England found themselves stranded when their aircraft, operated by Sakhaavia, failed to arrive for the homeward flight. For two nights the party was accommodated in Stansted Mountfitchet High School, which was opened specially as its students were on holiday, and the Emergency Planning Team from Uttlesford District Council provided beds and food. The Russians eventually took off for Yakutsk in Siberia on the night of 7 August.

Hijack — again!

Hardly had this problem been dealt with than Stansted was in the news again on 27 August, when the airport's well-rehearsed function as the 'designated' United Kingdom destination for hijacked aircraft was put to good effect. Airbus A.310-300 F-GKTD, on lease to Sudan Airways, had been taken over the previous evening by seven Iraqi dissidents during a flight from Khartoum to Amman in Jordan, Iraq's gateway to the outside world, and had landed instead at Larnaca in Cyprus to refuel. There, the Iraqis insisted that the pilot flew the Airbus to London. At 22.00 a warning of the possible outcome was sent to Stansted, and three hours later the airport was ready to receive the aircraft, with police and other forces in place. The Airbus touched down at

TODAY AND TOMORROW

Fighting the early morning half-light and a hand-held telephoto lens, Peter Smith manages to capture the Sudan Airways A310 F-GKTD parked on Compass Point in. The service stairs are ready for the first hostage release at 06.30am.

04.30 and was directed to the compass base, near to the FLS hangar and well away from the terminal building. By 06.30 ten hostages had been released, with more following until the last of the 180 passengers was freed at mid-day. The hijackers then emerged from the Airbus and were arrested, while the passengers, only one of whom was injured, were looked after by local authorities. During the operation at Stansted, the airport remained open except for three aircraft, but the effective length of useable runway was reduced so that other aircraft avoided passing close to the area where the Sudanese airliner was parked.

By September 1996 cargo business at Stansted had more than tripled since the cargo terminal opened in May 1989, over 100,000 tonnes, plus 10,000 tonnes of mail, having been handled in a year. A further extension, covering 32280 sq. ft. (3000 sq. m.) had been completed recently for use by Royal Mail and handling company GHI.

At the end of October 1996, Air UK's Rotterdam route was taken over by Suckling Airways, which several years previously had used Stansted as a terminus for a short time before settling at Cambridge. This family run airline - operated by Roy and Merlyn Suckling - increased their use of Stansted when one of their Dornier 328s began flying a francise-style service on behalf of Air UK to Zurich. New destinations for the winter 1996/97 season were Turin, to where Crystal Holidays began flying skiers on 15 December 1996, and Inverness, an addition to Air

A new sight at Stansted in 1997 was Suckling Airways' Dornier 328 G-BWIR, flown in an all-white colour scheme but with Air UK titling and used on the latters Stansted - Zurich service. [Simon Peters]

THE STANSTED EXPERIENCE

Flying the flag! A line-up of Air UK's Fokker 100's parked outside the International satellite, looking into the evening sun.
[Air UK]

UK's services. Frequencies were increased on the Air UK Copenhagen, Dusseldorf and Zurich routes on weekdays, and to Aberdeen, Edinburgh, Glasgow and Newcastle at weekends, meeting increased demands. Other new destinations were Lourdes, for three-day pilgrimages, and day trips to Budapest, Lapland and Warsaw with Airtours International were available.

Early in 1997 it was announced that two airlines which had not previously used Stansted were to do so - Cyprus Airways with a weekly flight to Larnaca and Azzura Air, with a scheduled weekend service to Bergamo in Italy, coincidentally the other end of the fruit-carrying service commenced almost exactly fifty years earlier, on 6 June 1947 by London Aero & Motor Services direct from Stansted!

Air UK planned to increase its six daily flights to Amsterdam to eight, while Jersey European stepped up its Belfast route to four flights per day. Luxair's serivce to Luxemburg was increased to two daily trips, and Ryanair planned to inaugurate new services to Kerryand Stockholm. Passenger figures for 1996 had shown a continuing increase, 23.7% more being handled than in 1995, and the significant 5 million passengers per year throughput was within sight.

On the cargo area, an extension to the building allowed Royal Mail to move into more spacious surroundings. Handling agent GHI Stansted had, by February 1997, increased its cargo area by half to give 3000 sq. m. (32280 sq.

ft.) of space. Stansted thus became Britain's third largest cargo airport.

The future
During the years to running uo to 2008, Stansted Airport Ltd. plans to spend over £100 million on more facilities in order to keep pace with foreseen demand. These developments will create a further 7000 jobs to add to today's 5000. Passengers are predicted to increase to 8 million in 2002 and 15 million in 2008. To cope with these figures, permission is needed for a greater number of aircraft movements, while enlargement of the terminal building to absorb land, currently vacant, on either side, and the construction of two further satellite buildings, will be necessary. Off-airport, a considerable increase in the local housing stock would be needed. Essex County Council's plan for improving the A120 road would need to be activated, and proposals exist for widening the M11 motorway north of the Stansted intersection, junction 8.

As this history appears in print, Stansted Airport approaches the major milestone of its five millionth passenger in a given twelve-month period, due to occur in May 1997. Perhaps the last word of this narrative can be left with Deana Frost, who escorts many of the British Airports Authority provided guided tours around the airport; *"...the airport at Stansted may have been under-used for years; but now the new infrastructure is in place, the facilities are superb and the future looks bright!"*

Chapter Nine

Epilogue

by

Dr. N. Brian Smith, Chairman BAA plc.

As you will have read in this superb book, when BAA plc was formed on August 1st 1986, Stansted's destiny as the third major airport for London had already been determined, following the approval the previous year of its development to handle 15 million passengers a year.

This was no mean feat after the years of uncertainty stretching back to the end of the second world war, but with Stansted's future looking assured efforts could be focused on getting the development built.

At the time, former Chairman Sir Norman Payne promised a meeting of airline representatives that the development of the airport would "*...provide an exciting and innovative new terminal building*".

The British Airports Authority's brief to the architect Sir Norman Foster had been for an efficient, cost-effective and "joyful" building. Calm, clarity and convenience were the key words. A Terminal specifically designed for the then highly regulated environment of London's airports, which guaranteed future traffic growth for the airport.

Prior to the opening of the terminal over 8,000 travel trade people toured the new site in project Vision, which included a futuristic film show. Most of these were travel agents who expected their package holiday clients would have no choice but to use the new airport as charters moved over from Gatwick.

All will agree that when Her Majesty the Queen opened the splendid new terminal on March 17th 1991 it did indeed fulfil the expectations of that challenging brief to the architect. But the expected demand for its facilities of a decade before was not there.

Unfortunately, what could not have been foreseen was the relaxation of 45 years of post war traffic distribution between the London airports, the start of an economic recession in the UK, which was to become one of the worst since the nineteen thirties, and the short term impact of a war in the Gulf, which dissuaded many people from flying.

The 1990/1 annual report of the Air Transport Users Committee notes that the year was the "*...toughest and most turbulent experienced by the air transport industry since the second world war*".

The Association of European Airlines saw short and medium haul international traffic plunge by 30 per cent in February 1990, while on the North Atlantic demand on some routes fell by over 50 per cent.

BAA therefore found itself in a situation it never had to face before; it had to market one of its airports. And market an airport that had had a turbulent track record to an airline industry whose immediate concern in 1991 was its very survival.

Some airlines did not make it and the collapse of the International Leisure Group and Air Europe only added to Stansted's challenge, as the very traffic it was built for, namely the charter business, consolidated back to traditional bases at Gatwick and Luton.

Stansted therefore had to find its Unique Selling Proposition and all credit must be given for the determination of everyone at airport as they took on the challenge of growing the business in an uncertain world.

Within a year of the opening of the terminal the airport had doubled its passenger traffic, and over the next six years Stansted maintained the fastest annual growth rate of any major UK airport.

THE STANSTED EXPERIENCE

From having just over one million passengers and handling around 33,000 tonnes of freight annually at the end of March 1991, Stansted has grown to over five million passengers and 110,000 tonnes of freight a year, making it the UK's sixth largest airport for passenger traffic and number three for freight.

All this, together with tight financial control, led to the airport coming into profit during the current financial year.

Ever since its conception in 1942, the story of Stansted has been about the future, and this is ever more so today, as we continue to witness unceasing demand for air travel and the pressure on our well established south-east gateways at Heathrow and Gatwick.

To keep pace with this ever-increasing business, BAA is spending a million pounds a day on building airport infrastructure. We believe it makes both business and environmental sense to make the fullest use of existing runway capacity.

This year, for the first time, airlines are finding it difficult to obtain the right take off and landing slots at Gatwick as well as Heathrow, indicating that Stansted will at last start to fulfil its original purpose as we enter to 21st century.

However, rather than the expected charter base the airport now offers a predominately scheduled service and has gained increasing popularity with business passengers. In fact, over 36 per cent of Stansted passengers are on business journeys - a higher percentage than Gatwick.

And Stansted is certainly not an alternative to the proposed Terminal 5, which is needed to ensure we can continue to offer our passengers at Heathrow the quality of service and level of comfort they expect as that airport reaches the capacity of its runways.

The new Stansted was designed with the future in mind, with facilities phased to provide them in a timely manner as and when demand dictated, thereby not only keeping overheads down, but also ensuring flexibility to meet charging requirements.

With Stansted a third of the way towards the limit of its present outline planning consent, we will shortly be seeing the completion of its second satellite building and work starting on its third, together with extensions to the terminal and eventually the fourth satellite.

Given our experience with Gatwick the capacity of Stansted's single runway is up to 40 million passengers per annum, but a second terminal will be required if we are to tap its full potential.

It is inevitable that the planning application for this proposal will involve a public enquiry, which like those before it will, I am sure, weigh up the national importance of utilizing the asset of Stansted with the concerns of the immediate local community.

The Stansted story is therefore far from over, and there are more exciting times ahead for the airport and those that work there. In another fifty years' time will a future Chairman of the British Airports Authority be writing a postscript to another book on Stansted and what history will that relate? Will it be as eventful as the airport's first fifty years?

I expect it will.

Abbreviations

ACHU	Aircrew Holding Unit	HPR	Handley Page (Reading)
ADF	Automatic Direction Finder	HQ	Headquarters
ADG	Air Depot Group	HS	Hawker Siddeley
An.	Antonov	IAS	
ANA	Australian National Airways	Il.	Ilyushin
APEX	Advance Purchase Excursion	ILS	Instrument Landing System
ATEL	Aviation Trading & Engineering Ltd.	Insp.	Inspector [of police]
ATL	Aviation Traders Ltd.	IRA	Irish Republican Army
ATP	Advanced Turbo-Prop	IT	Inclusive Tour
ATR		JAT	Jugoslav Air Transport
BAA	British Airports Authority	JEA	Jersey European Airways
BAC	British Aircraft Corporation	Ju.	Junkers
BADA	Base Air Depot Area	kg.	kilograms
BAe	British Aerospace	KLM	Koninklijke Luchvaart Maatschappij
BAF	British Air Ferries		NV (the national airline of Holland)
BEA	Britsh European Airways	km.	kilometres
Bf.	Bayerische Flugzeugwerke	Lab.	Labour
BG	Bomb Group	LAC	Lancashire Aircraft Corporation
Bn.	Battalion	LACS	
BOAC	British Overseas Airways Corporation	LAMS	London Aero & Motor Services Ltd.
		Lib.	Liberal
BoBMF	Battle of Britain Memorial Flight	LOT	Polskie Linie Lotnicze
Brig. Gen.	Brigadier General	LST	Landing Ship (Tank)
BS	Bomb Squadron	Lt.	Lieutenant
BUA	British United Airways	Lt. Col.	Lieutenant Colonel
CAA	Civil Aviation Authority	LTU	Luft Transport Union
CAFU	Civil Aviation Flying Unit	m.	metres
Capt.	Captain	MA	Master of Arts
CASA	Construcciones Aeronàuticas SA	Maj.	Major
CB	Companion of the Order of the Bath	MEK	Methyl-ethyl-ketone
CBI	Confederation of British Industries	MoA	Ministry of Aviation
CBW	Combat Bombardment Wing	MoCA	Ministry of Civil Aviation
CLA	Country Landowners Association	MP	Member of Parliament
CMG	Companion of the Order of St. Michael and St. George	MR&RS	Mobile Repair & Reclamation Squadron
CO	Commanding Officer	MT	Motor Transport
CofA	Certificate of Airworthiness	MU	Maintenance Unit
Col.	Colonel	NAAFI	Navy, Army & Air Force Institute
Con.	Conservative	NASA	National Air & Space Administration
DC	Douglas Commercial	NATO	North Atlantic Treaty Organisation
Det.	Detachment	NCO	Non-Commissioned Officer
DH	de Havilland	plc	Public Limited Company
DHC	de Havilland Canada	PoW	Prisoner of War
DL	Deputy Lieutenant	PX	Post Exchange
DME	Distance Measuring Equipment	QC	Queen's Counsel
Do.	Dornier	RAF	Royal Air Force
Dr.	Doctor	RAuxAF	Royal Auxiliary Air Force
DSO	Distinguished Service Order	RCAF	Royal Canadian Air Force
EA Bn	Engineer Aviation Battalion	RDC	Rural District Council
F	Fokker	Rev.	Reverend
Flt. Lt.	Flight Lieutenant	RNZAF	Royal New Zealand Air Force
1st. Lt.	First Lieutenant	ROMBAC	ROMania British Aircraft Corporation
FSTS	Fire Service Training School		
ft.	feet	RTPI	Royal Town Planning Institute
HP	Handley Page	SAS	Scandinavian Airlines System

SAS	Special Air Service		TWA	Trans World Airlines
SBAC	Society of British Aircraft		UDC	Urban District Council
	Constructors		UHF	Ultra high frwquency [radio]
sq.	square		UNRRA	United Nations Relief &
sq. ft.	square feet			Rehabilitation Administration
sq. m.	square metres		UPS	United Parcels Services
Sqn.	Squadron		USAAF	United States Army Air Force
Sqn. Ldr.	Squadron Leader		USAF	United States Air Force
TAC	Transmeridian Air Cargo		V	Vickers
TAD	Tactical Air Depot		Ven.	Venerable
TAP	Transportes Aereos Portugueses		VHF	Very High Frequency (radio)
TAT	Touraine Air Transport		VOR	Voice Omni-directional Radio Range
Tech. Sgt.	Technical Sergeant		WAAF	Women's Auxiliary Air Force
TGWU	Transport & General Workers Union		Wg. Cdr.	Wing Commander
Tu.	Tupolev			